NO BODY'S PERFECT
Dealing with Food Problems

Jasbindar Singh and Pat Rosier

Attic Press

Dublin

First Published in 1989 by
New Women's Press Ltd
New Zealand

First Published in Ireland in 1990 by
Attic Press
44 East Essex Street
Dublin 2

British Library Cataloguing in Publication Data
Singh, Jasbindar
    Nobody's perfect. -2nd. ed.
    1. Man. Appetite disorders
    I. Title   II. Rosier, Pat   III. Series
    616.8526

    ISBN 1-85594-007-8

Cover Design: Concept: Brenda McArdle
Drawings: Helen Courtney
Typesetting: Rennies Illustrations Ltd
Printing: The Guernsey Press Company Ltd.

Contents

Introduction 5

1 The problems: what are they? 13

2 Getting started 30

3 Food for thought 47

4 Coping with feelings 56

5 Body image and self-esteem 74

6 Relationships 86

7 Creating a new pathway 97

8 Self-help groups 103

9 For partners, friends and relations 106

Footnotes 109

Resources 110

Acknowledgements

This book is dedicated to the women who shared their stories and experiences because they wanted to help other women.

Our heartfelt thanks to all those who read the manuscript and gave us feedback: Ann Elborn, Sue Fitchett, Jeannette Forde, Hilary Haines, Miranda Jakich, Sue Louise, and Jane Sweeney. Their comments were a valuable contribution.

We also thank the following: Auburn Centre team for their support and understanding; John Gribben for help with statistical information; Cilla Potter and the Ranfurly community for sharing their insights on emotional and spiritual growth; the Mental Health Foundation for their support for Jasbindar's research; Linda Cassells, our original editor, for her invitation to write this book. We drew on the work of Agnes and John Sturt in the sections on feelings, anger, conflict, stress and spirituality. Finally, a very special thanks to Hilary, Richard and Kuldip for their love and support.

Introduction

Why a book on eating disorders?

Jasbindar

In my work as a clinical psychologist at a community mental health centre, I have realized that there are many women having problems with their weight and body image, as large numbers of women enquire about help for eating disorders, particularly bulimia. Often they ask if there is something they can read that would be more helpful than the advice they have been getting. ('You'll just grow out of it', 'Take these anti-depressants – or diet pills.') For the women who come for counselling, the single most common factor is an obsession with food arising from their concern about their body image and weight. This has led them to try diet after diet, which works for a while, but they put the weight back on and end up in a struggle with themselves, feeling out of control around food. It dominates their lives, and their fears about their bodies are accentuated.

In my counselling work I have become more and more aware of the pressures on women to be slim, to conform to an 'ideal' body image. Why do we internalize this pressure and take it so seriously? It has to do with our roles in society – the emphasis on women's appearance, the rewards we get for looking 'right' and the encouragement and approval we get for pleasing behaviour.

I have also become aware of what a struggle it is for women, psychologically, to strive for the perfect body, which is an unattainable ideal. It doesn't actually exist. But instead of seeing this, women blame themselves and see it as a personal failure that they can't achieve it, demonstrating a lack of will-power. This leads to a continual struggle with food in a love/hate relationship.

I have found that overcoming eating disorders can't be achieved overnight. It requires some soul searching and attitudinal changes, but it can be done. Because of the secrecy that surrounds women's problems with food, I

5

decided to write about the issues and ideas that women have found helpful. A book can be used privately, and since so many are struggling on their own, an emphasis on self-help support was vital.

Most of the material and information in this book has come from my research, in which about five hundred women responded to a questionnaire on bulimia[1], and from women I have seen in counselling. I wanted to produce a book based on the experiences of women, which could be available to those struggling with eating disorders in isolation, whether from fear of facing the problem, a reluctance to seek help, or geographical circumstances.

Pat

My interest in eating disorders was stimulated by my contact with women in community women's studies courses, where I found that any material about body image, fashion or dieting had a compelling interest for women of all ages, incomes and sizes. And as I read more theoretical books about women's roles and society's expectations of women, it increasingly made sense of my own life, as someone who is 'fat'.

When I wrote an article on 'Fighting Fat Phobia' for *Broadsheet* magazine, there was a huge response. For me, a surprising aspect of that response was the number of women who had never considered themselves to be fat who commented on how important the issues in the article were to them. I became aware of the pervasive nature of fear of fat, how *all* women in our society are affected by it.

In travelling to provincial centres to take part in seminars on women's health and related topics, I have become very aware of the isolation of women outside the main centres. Counselling is simply not a practical proposition for so many. So I see this book as an outreach, to women like Jane (below) and to all the women for whom food has become an obsession and an enemy rather than a pleasure.

Jane's story

'I started dieting in August 1987. I don't really know why – I guess it was a combination of insecurity and depression. I figured that if I was slimmer I'd like myself better. I mean, if I couldn't accept myself, how could others accept me?' 'I cut

down to very few calories a day and lost some weight very quickly. My obsession with calories increased and by December I was consuming less and less daily. I was starting to miss the sweet things. One day in early January I couldn't stand it any longer and went and bought cake, chocolate, ice-cream, potato chips. I sat down and binged out, until I couldn't move. That was the start of my anorexia turning to bulimia. I was so full I remember clearly the panic I felt. I didn't know what to do. I hopped on the scales and my weight had gone up. Out of complete fear and desperation I stuck my fingers down my throat and vomited it all up. Afterwards I remember feeling so relieved, but so guilty, ashamed and disgusted with myself. But from then on I knew that I could eat sweet things again by purging afterwards.

'Although I live alone, the thing that I find hardest is the deceitfulness. During the week at work people ask me why I'm not eating and I have to lie to them. Other days, I'm stuffing the food down and then leave the lunch room twenty minutes earlier so that I can go to the loo and vomit. I'll go without food for one or two days, then binge two to seven times in one day, costing me heaps in laxatives and up to £100 a week.

'I'm well aware of the consequences and the seriousness of anorexia and bulimia but somehow that doesn't seem as important as my need to binge and lose weight. Plus, since my periods have stopped, I feel as though I have control over my body and my life. For the first time in my life I feel in control. My weight is way down but I still feel very fat and bulgy. I have stopped socializing almost completely because I feel that people are always looking at how fat I am. I am withdrawn and suffer from a lot of depression, am extremely tired during the day but can't sleep at night.

'I have resigned myself to the fact that I am bulimic. I guess in a way I have given up trying to stop the bingeing because I know that to stop and try to resume a normal lifestyle would mean putting on weight. That's a step I'm not ready to take. Maybe one day I'll be able to.

'There are only two people, other than Jasbindar, who know about my bulimia. They are people I work with, one of whom I feel particularly close to and can trust – I have found that talking about it seems to help. But I can see

7

that it's hurting her because she doesn't know what to say or do. I don't think there's anything – just love me!'

The three strands of eating disorders

Our approach in this book is based on our belief that there are three strands to eating disorders – social/cultural (what is expected of us as women); emotional/psychological (our feelings about ourselves, our relationships); and physical (the interaction between our genetic make-up and what we do or don't eat). Separating these out from each other is in some ways false, as they are interwoven. However, it is also necessary to recognize each one as significant in itself. Much writing on eating disorders has tended to focus on one (perhaps most often the emotional/psychological) and under-play the role of the others. We believe that overcoming an eating disorder involves dealing with all three. We discuss them in more detail in Chapter 1.

Is this book for me?

We believe that all women are affected by the pressure to be thin, whether they are heterosexual, lesbian, young, old, rich, poor, dark, fair, thin, fat, healthy, sick, have a disability, are single, with a partner, or any combination of these.

If you have any sort of struggle with food, worry about being or getting fat, or are preoccupied with your body image, we believe *No Body's Perfect* has something for you.

For many women, preoccupation with body size has not been an intrinsic part of their culture, and a hugh range of sizes is normal and okay. Although many cultures do not traditionally focus on women's body size as a source of their identity, women from all cultures, particularly younger ones, are increasingly affected by the values of Western society, including the ideal of thinness.

Anorexia seems most often to start in the early teens, and bulimia in the later teens. Anorexia has been found in girls under ten. In Jasbindar's study[2] eighty-five per cent of the bulimic women had symptoms by the time they were eighteen. While anorexia and bulimia are two extremes on a continuum, most of us can place ourselves somewhere on that line, particularly when we take into account obsessive thinking about food. Many of us diet only occasionally and never actually consider ourselves fat, but talk about 'getting fat' as a constant anxiety. This in itself distorts our relationship with food and creates guilt and other bad feelings around dieting. We also use food as a comfort to help us cope with strong feelings and this, too, creates a distortion.

We hope that *No Body's Perfect* will reach women who have any sort of problem with food, dieting, weight or body image, and give them some guidelines for change. More and more women are identifying themselves to counsellors and support groups as needing help. They will find the ideas and exercises in this book useful. The issues that we address (such as moving away from a diet mentality, developing an identity in terms broader than just the physical, and exploring underlying feelings, as well as looking at behaviour with food) are relevant to *all* eating disorders, including anorexia.

Since we want to take the focus off weight, we decided not to mention in the text specific weights, numbers of laxatives used, or actual weight loss or gain. Women who have been thinking in these terms ('I lost/gained xx kilos today/this week') for a long time find it difficult to get out of the habit of making comparisons. We did not want to encourage the habit. Our aim is to help women develop healthy eating patterns and a life free from food and size obsessions.

This book will help you explore the underlying factors that affect your eating – just trying to change your eating patterns is not effective. There are no magic cures. The healing process tends to be slow, and sometimes painful. But the rewards are enormous.

The stories in the text are from women who have written to Jasbindar, completed the questionnaire she used for her research, or offered their experience when they knew we were writing the book. To preserve confidentiality, we have given each a randomly-selected name, but the stories are real.

How to use the book

The text is planned as a sequence and we suggest that you work through it from the beginning. However, you are in control. You may choose to focus on the topics in a different order – for example, some women have preferred to deal with body image and self-esteem before trying to change their eating patterns. Whichever, skim through and look at the headings and drawings to get an idea of the overall scope before you start.

Each chapter includes ideas, exercises and quotes from women who have experienced problems with food. All of these are important for self-help. An estimate of the time needed for each exercise is provided – try to give uninterrupted time to them. If it feels useful, go back and repeat earlier exercises (particularly those that had a powerful impact on you), and talk about them with friends. We see the book as a resource and would like it to be used in as many ways as possible.

Working through the book might arouse fears and anxieties which make you feel like not going on. These feelings are a natural part of any process of change. Let yourself experience them. You may also experience feelings of resistance, anger, or frustration. We suggest that you acknowledge these feelings and work through them. Maybe they come up each time you start a new project. If so, just recognize the feelings are there, and continue. The book will give you a chance to explore them – they may be related to your problems with food. If it feels like too much at times, slow down. Work through the chapters at your own pace, do the exercises more than once if you feel like it.

It can be a real help if you can set up some support for yourself, either with a friend who is using the book as well, or with a friend who is willing to support you.

Keeping a diary or journal to record exercises, thoughts and feelings can be valuable, whether you are working through the book on your own, with a friend or in a group. The act of writing your thoughts and feelings can help to clarify them and enable you to move on. A journal is something you keep for yourself – you are entitled to it as a private place that is 'for your eyes only'. You are writing for yourself, so it doesn't have to be a literary masterpiece! Or even correctly spelt! If you find keeping a journal difficult, try recording your responses to exercises on scraps of paper (then you can throw them away if you hate them!), or just think about them. If you adopt the thinking approach, make sure you allow enough time for your thoughts about each question in the exercise to become clear.

You may have had your particular difficulties with food for many years, so they will not disappear overnight. If you are bulimic, reducing the frequency of your bingeing and purging is as much a success as total abstention.

If you start to read the book and do the exercises, but find you just cannot carry on, don't berate yourself as a failure. It may be that you are not yet ready for the level of change needed. Think of it as a 'practice run', put it away for a while and come back to it when you feel 'ready'.

Christine's story

'Ever since I was thirteen I have been obsessed with food, dieting and my weight. And I am sick of it. I'm sick of waking up in the morning and wondering whether I'm going to make it through the day without bingeing. I'm sick of getting cramps in my stomach from taking too many laxatives. And I'm sick of crying into the toilet bowl after making myself sick and feeling like I've got no control over my life.

'I am twenty-one now and although I have come a long way in the last two years, I still feel like I'm not quite there. The times when I make myself sick are now few and far between and I have cut down my laxative intake. However, my compulsive eating still comes in waves and manages to smother me, and my obsession with food and weight is still strong, although these days it tends to be labelled 'health' rather than 'vanity'.

'I feel angry at society for imposing such ridiculous ideals of beauty on women. I feel angry at the media for exploiting these ideals, and I feel angry at me for somehow still believing that if I can't be slim and beautiful, I must in some way be inadequate. But deepest of all, I think, is the sadness and compassion I feel for all the women who can't accept themselves as they are, whether they be a size 10 or size 22, who are still trying to attain the perfect look. Unless they do, they see themselves as second-rate human beings.

'There is not one woman I know who feels totally at ease with the way she looks.'

Some questions to think about

Do you
- feel dissatisfied with your body?
- think your body would be fine if you could lose just a little weight?
- diet, take diet pills – or think about dieting a lot?
- think about food a lot of the time?
- feel out of control around food?
- exercise obsessively?
- use laxatives or vomiting to get rid of food you have eaten?
- try not to eat at all?
- worry about getting fat?

If you answer yes to any of these questions, we think our book has something to offer you. Bon voyage!

1 The problems: what are they?

Our three-strand approach to dealing with food problems involves social/cultural, emotional/psychological, and physical factors. In this chapter we will look at each strand in more detail.

Social/cultural aspects

APPEARANCE

In our culture there is an excessive focus on the way women look. Advertising, television programmes and films tend to portray women as more decorative and less active than men. (There is a saying, 'Women are, men do', which illustrates this.) Fashion is about what you look like, and the diet industry has a real interest in promoting an ever-slimmer ideal: it's called 'the profit motive'. Some fitness programmes also get on this bandwagon by confusing body fitness with appearance and promoting their programme as 'creating a slimmer, lovelier you'.

As women, we tend to be judged on externals – how we look and how we behave – that are defined by others. Throughout history, beautiful women have been admired, but in our century the criteria are becoming more difficult to meet. The last twenty years have seen beauty and 'centrefold' women in magazines like *Playboy* grow thinner and thinner, while the average weight of American women has increased. As the difference between the 'ideal' and reality gets greater, the pressure on all women increases.

We are judged by a yardstick of femininity, but we haven't set the standard of measurement. A look at women's magazines this century shows how the ideal 'real' woman promoted by them has changed with economic and social circumstances. For example, during World War Two, women were encouraged into heavy jobs (like armaments manufacturing and truck driving) because the men were overseas, yet after the war, when the men needed the jobs back, homemaking became the ideal. These days, we are expected to be 'superwomen', active in paid jobs and willing to carry the full burden of unpaid work at home and in the community. We blame ourselves when we fail to pull it off, and lose sight of who we are, and of our own feelings and needs.

BODY IMAGE

In terms of body image, the standards are arbitrary, too. A 1930s advertisement says, 'It's a *crime* to be skinny. They say I'm *twice* as pretty since I gained ten pounds' and advertises yeast and iron pills for weight gain. In the 1980s diet pills are advertised – for the weight loss currently promoted as desirable.

Those 'ideal' women in fashion magazines are just that. They are constructed – make-up, hair and clothes people hover around making constant adjustments to get the right 'look' (they even peg clothes at the back to make them hang a certain way). And many of the models have to constantly punish their bodies with exercise and diet to achieve their particular look. The camera 'fattens' models just as it fattens anyone, so they must be smaller than they appear on film.

The sort of person we are, our thoughts and feelings, values, skills and knowledge are not rated as highly as the way we look. As one sixteen-year-old said, 'If you're at a party and a pretty girl walks in, everyone turns their head and looks. Everybody wants to know her, to be her friend. But how can you know what she's really like just from looking at her?' Think about your own friends, and other people who are important to you. Are they close to you *because* of what they look like or because they have qualities that you love and admire? Yet maybe you continue to judge yourself by the way you 'appear'?

There is nothing inherently wrong with fashion, or exercise. What *is* wrong is the way the promoters of these industries use them to make us feel dissatisfied with the bodies we have. We are all dissatisfied with some aspect of our bodies as a result. And this is reinforced every day of our lives.

Because we become convinced that our bodies are the most important thing about us, losing weight and looking

They don't work but they do provide a sense of failure.

'right' are seen as a cure for all the things that are wrong in our lives. We also get the message that we can actually change our body size to whatever we want – that it's absolutely within our control. (The issue of control is a vital one for many women – see Jane's story, p. 6.) All you have to do is go on this new diet (and there are hundreds of weight-loss diets in existence) – and if it doesn't work then it's because you didn't do it properly or this particular diet didn't suit you – but another may! So you keep trying, reinforced by the little weight loss you may have achieved. What you are not told is that you will very likely put this weight back on and that ultimately *diets don't work*. According to Judy Norsigian of the Boston Women's Health Collective, ninety-nine per cent of women put the weight they lost on a diet back on within five years and ninety-five per cent put on more than they lost. For most of us there is a real see-saw or series of cycles – new diet, weight loss, off the diet, weight gain.[3]

What we are doing is believing the message that we can have the 'perfect' body if we can just get it 'right', just have enough will-power to stay on the latest diet (even if that means we are hungry for the rest of our lives!). This message is presented as the truth, even though it is based on a distortion of reality which has led us to think that we are not okay as we are.

FOOD

We also get double messages about food – on the one hand we are taught to plan, prepare and organize food for family and social occasions. We are the care-givers, the providers of food and nurturing. At the same time food is something that we have to be wary about for ourselves. If we 'indulge' we'll get fat! So food has a whole complex range of meanings for us – it's part of our social role, we probably enjoy it, but it's also a sin to 'indulge' ourselves.

Flicking through the pages of a women's magazine, we may see amazing recipes with pictures of mouth-watering food and, over the page, yet another diet, or a woman's story about how she lost weight, or a super-slim model, or all three. In the light of all this, it's hardly surprising that some of us develop eating disorders. Those of us with a severedisorder like anorexia, are denying ourselves food in our striving for perfection and control. If we are bulimic, we are bingeing and purging and using food to satisfy emotional needs. At the same time we hate ourselves for our 'weakness'.

We have an enormous fear of fat in Western society. We can be tolerant of it on others but are often phobic about it on ourselves. We have all heard women say things like, 'I shall feel so much better when I'm a kilo or two lighter', or 'I know I will look better in my clothes when I'm thinner'. One woman wrote to Jasbindar, 'I can remember thinking that if I had the perfect body, I would have the perfect life.'

Often, what we are fighting is our body's natural growth process. Susan put it like this: 'I have never been drastically overweight and was actually not overweight at all when I first started to diet. I was eighteen at the time and I realize now that I was just filling out and maturing.'

We explore these ideas further in Chapters 3, 4 and 5.

Emotional/psychological aspects

There is plenty of evidence that eating disorders are on the increase. American studies show that from five to twenty per cent of female college students are bulimic. An Auckland survey found that fourteen per cent of the fifteen hundred secondary school girls questioned displayed attitudes towards weight and eating that could lead to eating disorders. The researchers predicted that between three and eight per cent of them actually had eating disorders, either anorexia nervosa or bulimia.[4]

The New Zealand magazine survey conducted by Jasbindar[5] got responses from over five hundred women with questions about bulimia. Three hundred and fifty of the women completed a questionnaire because they identified themselves as bulimic. Some of the women are happy with their jobs, have reasonable living circumstances, and a good relationship. Others feel alone and isolated, and do not have close relationships. What they share is a fear of fatness, loss of control over eating, fears about their health, feeling bad about themselves, and depression.

These women are the tip of a huge iceberg – a lot of women who responded to Jasbindar's survey said they had a friend with similar problems. The shame, guilt and secrecy associated with food-related problems prevents many of us from acknowledging that we actually have a problem, let alone filling out a questionnaire or seeking help. As Christine wrote, 'Food is my one and only enemy, I find my problem embarrassing, depressing and I hate it.'

SELF-ESTEEM

Women who do not have good self-esteem are very vulnerable to eating disorders. How we feel about ourselves is how we are, it affects everything we do and say. If we are feeling good about ourselves, we interact with the world differently from the way we do when we are feeling bad about ourselves.

Our very early experiences in life have a strong influence on our self-esteem. However, if we have low self-esteem we are not stuck with it. We can learn to think and feel more positively about ourselves. See Chapter 5 for more on this.

FEELINGS

We all have emotional needs, but few of us learn that it is okay to expect to have these met. Feelings that we have not acknowledged to ourselves and not acted on tend to hang around and contribute to our feeling bad. One of the things that the women who took part in Jasbindar's survey referred to was using food to 'stuff down' strong feelings that they did not have other strategies for dealing with. 'Feeding the hungry heart' by raiding the pantry at night is not the only way to deal with feelings of loneliness, unhappiness, being unloved, depression, fear, guilt . . .

As women, many of us experience conflict around the roles and expectations placed on us by society and family. Again, food can be used to deal with these pressures. We may never have learnt that it's all right to have angry or negative feelings, without having to 'stuff' them down. There are better ways of dealing with these feelings than using food to blot them out, and we look at these in more detail in Chapter 4.

CONTROL

Control is another issue. Our body can be one area where we feel we can exercise free will and have some control. For example, an anorexic woman may decide to exceed the slim ideal by *totally* controlling her body and her hunger. This can be accompanied by a sense of resistance, or even defiance – whether to our family's expectations, to our bodies becoming mature and sexual, to growing up – that feels powerful and in control. However, this control is mythical, and in the long term can only be self-destructive. The ultimate control of the anorexic, which is to stop eating, can only lead to death. (There is a paradox here, in that the anorexia is in fact controlling the person.)

The demands of the body and some basic self-preservation instinct can trigger bingeing. Thus anorexia often leads to bulimia. Bingeing leads to feelings of losing control and the need to regain it by purging. And for those of us who manage to avoid the extremes of anorexia or bingeing, there are still control anxieties around food. We feel we must have self-control, we deny ourselves pleasurable eating, for fear of getting fat.

Physical aspects

It is very clear to us that the precondition for most eating problems is dieting. Food deprivation, which is the basis of most weight-loss diets, sets up a hunger that will eventually over-ride any other feelings, and lead to bingeing. As Jo wrote, 'I have been bingeing and vomiting since I was seventeen after my will-power to diet had exhausted itself.'

NATURAL WEIGHT

The fallacy that we can totally control our body size by control of what we eat is a common belief. Yet the opposing idea of a 'set point', which is the natural weight for each individual and which may be very different in people with the same height and bone structure, is now well established. 'According to this view, obesity for some individuals represents a "normal" or even an "ideal" body weight.'[6] Body size is determined by a number of different things – genetic make-up, metabolic rate, food intake, exercise, all of which contribute to a 'set point' which determines our body weight. It will remain fairly stable, regardless of what we do to try and change it.

Trying to get away from this weight results in the body setting up mechanisms (such as a lower metabolic rate) aimed at returning you to 'set point'. Repeated long-term diets train the body to deal with diets, by getting rid of some lean tissue and replacing it with the fat that is useful in starvation or famine conditions. Fat can provide energy and needs less fuel (food) than lean organs and muscle. So the metabolic rate of a dieter gets lower as the body adapts and you get *fatter* on less food than before.

There is a lot of individual variation in 'set point'; some people are naturally heavier and some naturally thinner. Most women's natural weight is well above the current ideal for feminine beauty.

CHANGE AND OUR BODIES

Our bodies change over time, from puberty, through the middle years, to menopause and old age. If we are fighting our natural body size, we will also end up fighting these changes. We can never actually control them – we will get old regardless of what we do to stop it showing!

Jasbindar's research has shown that most of the women were the same weight after years of bingeing and purging as they had been before they started. Bingeing and purging had become an escalating and vicious cycle, since vomiting allowed them to give in to their desire to eat without the fear of gaining weight. In fact, the original object of losing weight had failed.

In this book we deal with these physical aspects of eating disorders from two angles. One (and there's an obvious overlap with the psychological aspects here) involves a greater acceptance of our actual body size. The other concerns a return to more ordinary eating patterns – we cover this in detail in Chapter 3. If you do have any concerns for your physical health, get a thorough physical check-up from your doctor. Be wary of those doctors who don't listen to what you say, assume that you'll be okay if only you lose some weight, or don't believe in giving patients information that will worry them. Young women often find it hard to talk to the family doctor — it may be worth finding a doctor of your own, consulting the nearest women's health group or centre.

These, then, are the three strands which make up the theoretical basis of our self-help approach – the social/cultural, psychological/emotional, and the physical.

What is fat phobia?

Shona's definition: *'People say I look fit and trim, but I don't believe them and I always feel "fat" inside!'*

Paula put it like this: *'I am strongly feminist. I hate all the stereotyped images and models for women, yet I want to be slim. The real fear is of course being FAT!'*

For Ngaire, it's a huge conflict: *'I'm sixteen years old and have been bulimic for five years. I was hospitalized for three weeks last year. I hated every moment of it and was still vomiting all the time I was in hospital, while everyone thought I was making progress. I desperately wanted to make myself normal again but the fear of putting on weight was too great.'*

FEAR OF FAT

Fat phobia means fear of fat. For most of us the biggest fear is of being fat ourselves. But what is fat? Anyone bigger than size 12? 16? 18? There aren't any objective criteria, given the genetic factors and cultural differences. Yet for most of us in Western societies fat equals bad.

We start being ruled by height/weight charts the day we are born. As adults, we come across them mainly in doctors' rooms or in connection with insurance and some jobs (police force, modelling). In fact, there are more useful ways of measuring both health (for insurance companies) and fitness. Our own body performance, for example whether we puff going up a flight of stairs, will give a much more accurate measure of how healthy and fit we are. How far we can comfortably walk is another measure. Yet if we fall outside the 'recommended' weight for our height on an insurance company chart (and these are the source of the doctors' charts, too) we tend to think our bodies are somehow failing. Being healthy and reasonably fit is what matters, not whether we fit some artibrary formula.

Fat phobia affects us throughout our lives. This is what Sally said:

'I found that while I was pregnant there was a great emphasis on how much weight I had put on at each check-up. The pressure is on from the moment a child is born. The first question is what sex is the baby, the next one is how big? I experienced a lot of pressure after the birth of two nine-pound babies. Then it was Plunket – it seemed to me that the most important thing to the nurse was how big or small the child was. I have talked to other women like myself who felt quite anxious about our children's body image from when they were born.'

School children who are seen as fat by their peers are teased, left out, called lazy, dirty, sloppy, ugly, not someone you would have as a friend. Teachers, psychologists, nurses and doctors often share these attitudes, so the stereotypes start affecting us from a young age.

The disincentives for 'fat' children to be active and engage in physical exercise start really young. Fatness is identified as a health problem when often the problem can be society's attitude towards it; the health problems arising from crash diets and other attempts to control body size; or the social restrictions on fat people exercising.

It is important to distinguish between health and fitness. Many fat people, particularly those who have managed to avoid punishing diet cycles, are healthy, but because of the attitudes towards fat people and exercise it is very difficult for those of us who are fat to exercise enough to be fit (and it's difficult to get large-size shorts, track suits and so on).

SOME MYTHS ABOUT FATNESS

There are a lot of myths about fatness which many of us apply to ourselves – whether or not anyone thinks of us as fat. Again, professionals, friends, partners and family have learnt these myths as well as we have ourselves. Here's a sample selection:

Fat people eat more.
Fat people are lazy.
Fat people are happy, jovial, and don't mind being teased.
Fat people don't have any control over their appetites and lives.
Fat people don't work as hard.

Can you think of any other common beliefs about fat people?

In fact, as a group, fat people are as diverse as any other group. There are plenty of lazy thin people around, and some very active fat ones. Many thin people eat a lot more than many fat people. Fatness is often identified as a health problem, exactly how is seldom explained in detail, but many of us have experienced going to the doctor for advice and treatment on anything from cystitis to infertility to depression and being advised to 'lose some weight'. Maybe we've been given a little calorie chart. Or even diet pills. All worse than useless.

Judy Norsigian of the Boston Women's Health Collective has written: 'There are certainly health risks associated with

22

excessive fatness, including an increased risk of uterine cancer, high blood pressure, and diabetes. Many problems may be unfairly blamed on fatness, since so many studies have included only those fat people who have been on constant diets. It is not clear in those instances whether we are measuring the risks of being fat as opposed to the risks of chronic dieting. Many fat people who do not diet, but who do exercise regularly, are extremely healthy people.

'There are also risks associated with thinness. The major reason why unusually thin people tend to die young is increased cancer risk. Thinner people are also more susceptible to emphysema, fatal infections such as tuberculosis and other problems such as ulcers, anaemia, and osteoporosis. Also, thin women are much more likely to give birth to premature or underdeveloped babies . . .

'What about the benefits of extra body fat? First we survive trauma better because of more body reserves. Second, menopause may be a gentler transition because of the oestrogen production that takes place in fat tissue. Third, carrying around some extra weight can help to prevent osteoporosis because of the bone strengthening caused by extra body mass. In one famous study (Framingham heart study) the women with the lowest mortality rates were 10-30 per cent over the ideal weights on the insurance tables.'

In fact, what damages our health is repeated attempts at weight loss, and consequent weight gain, a cycle that can cause extreme stress on body organs and lead to later health problems. It's much healthier (although excruciatingly difficult for many of us!) to accept the body size we are.

Sexual and emotional abuse

Experience of abuse at any point in your life can destroy your sense of worth and control. Jasbindar found in her research that one third of the bulimic women responding had been sexually abused, according to their own definition. Over half of these had been abused before they were ten, and many had been abused more than once. Eighty-seven to ninety-two percent knew the perpetrator and half of these were family members such as fathers, step-fathers, grandfathers, uncles. Few of these bulimic women indicated in their stories that they had sought any help for the abuse.

It is not surprising that a woman who has had the most personal and vulnerable territory of her body violated ends up being anorexic, bulimic, or with some other self-destructive behaviour (e.g. drug or alcohol addiction).

It is even worse when someone who has been abused has attempted to tell and been met with disbelief or 'It must have been your fault' reactions. No young girl or woman asks to be raped and the abuse of power by the adult is totally the adult's responsibility.

Food is used to stuff down and dampen uncomfortable feelings that are too painful to confront or deal with. The fulfilling and nurturing qualities of food quench the pain and emotional hunger, but only temporarily. It's no wonder that a sexually abused woman grows up with the message that her body is not her own or is filthy or undesirable; or that she is just a body and nothing else. Many bulimic women, whether or not they have been sexually abused, encounter this split between their 'self' and their body. 'If only my body would do what I tell it to'. The body becomes the enemy of the self with a will of its own.

Self-esteem is enhanced when we can see our bodies and our 'selves' as part of the same worthwhile whole. Women who have been sexually abused will find it helpful to explore the abuse, no matter how long ago it occurred. Counselling, with a woman counsellor experienced in sexual abuse, or joining a survivors group are the best options. If neither of these is possible, there are a number of books that can be helpful (see Resources). Dealing with the abuse may be extremely painful but women find, overwhelmingly, that it shifts them from feeling like a victim, not in control of her life, to a survivor who has reclaimed her power and strength.

Why women rather than men?

Although a few men develop severe eating problems, by far the largest numbers of those affected are women. Men tend to use other means – such as alcohol – to blot out feelings.

The reasons for problems with food affecting women rather than men are complex. Women are the target for many consumption messages in our society – particularly through television and magazine advertising. The food industry certainly aims a lot of its advertising at women. On the whole, it is women who write shopping lists and make decisions about food, plan meals and go shopping – and a lot of this activity is focused on meeting other people's needs. But we are supposed to deny ourselves the pleasure of eating freely because it might make us fat.

OUR BODIES ARE BIG BUSINESS

Other aspects of the consumer society that are focused on women are the fashion, make-up and diet industries. These are multi-billion dollar industries that have a big investment in convincing us that our bodies are not okay as they are, and that we should use *their* products to make them 'right' and acceptable. These promotions have been so successful that, for many women, dieting has become a social norm ('Everybody does it'). It has become so much a part of women's lives that it is often not seen as the tyranny it is.

In the media the most sought-after woman is depicted as thin and stereotypically attractive, and all the better if she has the right statistics in the right places. Women's bodies are presented as units to be changed or altered at random. They are reduced, shrunk, even cut down to an ideal size which is presented as the only way to be, leaving thousands of women feeling ashamed and guilty because somehow they will never make it. Models' bodies are arranged and manipulated and lighting and camera angles are finely adjusted to achieve a desired 'effect' which even they cannot maintain, except for that instant in front of the camera. One advertisement for jeans had the image of an already thin model elongated to an impossible thinness by stretching the photograph. The fantasy of what women 'should' look like, some fashion photographer or promotor's ideal, is presented as real.

Bodies are also presented as a collection of bits. Witness the long, slim legs in the panty-hose ad, the elongated thigh and super-flat stomach in the swimming togs ad, the long neck and perfectly smooth shoulders in the perfume ad. In fact, one ad showing different bits features a number of models – and the legs and stomach often don't belong to the same person.

Contestants in beauty contests are often very like each other. Take a look at the women around you next time you are in the supermarket – we are actually a lot of different shapes and sizes. Where are the models who reinforce this diversity and the advertising that presents positive and real images that reflect the way we actually are? Buried under the drive for profits. We are made to feel dissatisfied with our bodies so that we can be sold 'hope' in the form of products: this brand of pantyhose will make your legs look 'perfect'; that brand of make-up will enable you to look as though you have ideal features; these diet pills will help you attain the perfect, slim body. We don't get told that our largish calf muscles are excellent for the tramping we love, or that our features are okay and don't need to be distorted into an illusion of something else, or that the diet pills won't give us an ideal body shape, but will kill our normal experience of hunger, and may well have other side-effects.

FOOD PROVIDERS

As food providers, most of us are familiar with the 'burnt-chop' syndrome, where we give the 'best' food to everyone else, and serve ourselves with what is left. In traditional Indian families whether or not there is plenty of food, the mother puts her husband and children first and herself last when it comes to apportioning food. Without being aware of it, many of us assume that men and boys need more food than girls and women, and dish up food accordingly. This probably arises from a combination of men and boys being seen as the 'workers' who need the nourishment because they are doing more physical things and bring in the money, and our own fears of eating too much.

REINFORCING MESSAGES

It is true that we feel 'better' when we lose weight. We get positive reinforcement from other people, we feel better in our clothes because we are closer to the ideal. (And if we are one of the optimists who buy clothes that are a bit small because we plan to lose the weight that will make them fit, our clothes will actually become more comfortable.) This shows how much women's sense of identity is based on external criteria. Most people are too polite to comment when the weight goes back on but many of us have had male partners who have managed to convey, openly or subtly, that

26

they feel much better being out with us when we are slimmer. Some even make comments about us 'putting a bit on' or ask 'should you be eating that?' We have to deal with their hang-ups (they get the same messages that we do) about our body size, as well as our own.

The points made above help to explain why we can get caught up in conflicts about ourselves, our body image and food. Problems with food are a response to the conflicting messages and internal emotional conflicts we have been discussing that lead to loss of self-esteem for women.

Julie's story

'I am thirty-three years old. I was the middle child of a family of three.

'As a child I was rather quiet and shy and tended to keep in the background. I spent a lot of time hanging around and tagging after my brother. I was always a bit tubby. I used to enjoy most food.

'I was slightly overweight at secondary school and for the first couple of years as a tertiary student. I lost a little weight in my early twenties, just by reducing my food input. It wasn't until just before going on a holiday abroad that I actually tried one of those fad diets. I thought it would be nicer to be slim while I was away. I tried the Israeli Army Diet which I managed for the first three to four days before finding myself becoming very tired and a bit light-headed. Commonsense took over and I stopped. Even so, I did lose enough weight to make me happy. This I kept off while away and through to the next winter.

'Here is my first recollection of bingeing and purging (ten years ago). I remember going to a party, having already eaten well, and then finding myself eating heaps more food. It wasn't long before I went to the toilet and let it all come up. (I discovered I regurgitate really easily.) From then on I kept purging, more so than bingeing. I only binged on odd occasions.

'I think I became disheartened that I had put the weight back on and all of a sudden I found a way to control things.

'With purging like this, plus the fact that I had become very keen on jogging, I actually lost a lot of weight and became quite slim. I was living at home all this time, until I went on a working holiday overseas. The previous summer I had injured my hip while playing sport. This prevented my doing any exercise, even jogging, for the two years I was away. Therefore, one of my ways of controlling my weight disappeared.

'Experiencing the joys of travel, including food and drink, I put on quite a lot of weight. I think this is when I started to binge, partly because I had left home and I was in charge of myself and the food I bought, so therefore I could binge whenever I wanted.

'Not that I did it a lot, that was yet to come. I still tended to purge more than binge. The fact that I had put on weight, plus sometimes felt homesick, resulted in my getting quite depressed at times. This, then seemed to be when I turned to food.

'On my return home I found it hard to settle. I had become more independent, yet I was supposed to be the same as I was two years before. This eventually improved when I went flatting, and then moved into a home of my own. I now have a certain amount of independence but still have the closeness of my family which I need.

'I had a job lined up on my return to New Zealand. However, the position is not challenging me any more, and

28

actually hasn't been for a long time. I have no mental stimulation. I find it can get me down very easily, and before I know it I end up on a bingeing and purging cycle.

'*Living on my own doesn't necessarily help the situation, because it is much easier to continue or start the cycle. In 1984 I tried to come to grips with the bulimia. I went to my GP, had a long talk with him and then ended up seeing a psychologist. He was very nice but, even though I tried to a certain extent, I don't think I was ready. I ended up cheating and got nowhere. I then tried hypnotherapy and this also proved no help. From 1984 until early this year I have done nothing about seeking further help. Instead I just kept bingeing and purging more and more until I was so fed up with myself.*

'*Around Christmas I went to a woman counsellor. This was the first time I was able to really talk to someone and feel that I was being understood. This alone has been a major plus for me as I have never been able to talk about my problem and it's hard to keep it bottled up inside for years and years.*'

As you work through this book keep the three strands – social/cultural, emotional/psychological, and physical – in mind. It will remind you that your problem with food is not just your individual hang-up, that larger social issues are also involved.

Good luck!

2   Getting Started

We start this chapter with the stories of two women that may
reflect aspects of your life. One has begun to make some
changes by joining a group, the other is at a point where she
wants to change. Your experience may be different, but you
do share a desire to do something about your problem with
food. These stories are two out of hundreds that Jasbinder
has received in response to magazine articles and her
research. You are certainly not alone, either in having a
problem with food, or in wanting to change it.

   The stories are followed by a group of exercises to start
you thinking about your own patterns around food.

Raewyn's story

'My problem began when I left New Zealand to travel
overseas when I was 21. Up until then I considered myself to
have a normal eating pattern. I was perhaps a bit overweight
but was never really bothered about it. Certainly not as
obsessed as I later became.

   'After being overseas a few months, I gained a few pounds
because of the lifestyle we were living, so I decided to go on a
diet. I can remember something seemed to click in my head
and I became very strict with myself, hardly eating anything.
I couldn't believe how easy it seemed to lose weight. I got
down to a weight which I though was fantastic – I could
wear the latest fashion then, skin-tight jeans. I remember
feeling odd, though, as if it wasn't really me who was thin –
it was somebody else's body.

   'When I finally stopped dieting I found I couldn't eat
normally. I was eating all sorts of rubbish, but never in front
of anybody. I would have my usual rabbit food in front of
other people and then run down to the shop and gorge on
chocolate bars, etc. The problem quickly became worse and I
spent the next two years overseas starving and bingeing.

   'Before returning to New Zealand, I tried desperately to
come back as the new, thin, me, but that only resulted in my
becoming fatter than ever. I returned to my home town, and

thought a complete change would be the solution, so moved to the city.

'I spent the next five years bingeing and starving and thinking of nothing but food. I was completely obsessed with my weight and would make charts and all sorts of goals to reach. I tried Weight Watchers, acupuncture, hypnotherapy, all with no success. I never admitted my problem to anyone, partly because I didn't understand it myself. My friends must have thought something was wrong, though, because I never ate in front of them, and told lies and made up all sorts of excuses not to go out because I felt so fat and revolting.

'The few times I did lose weight I was terrified to go out anyway, in case I gained weight again. Once again I thought a change would cure me, so I moved yet again to another city.

'Of course, it didn't make any difference. I took a night-time job and it was easy not to face anybody over a meal table. I was never able to make myself sick, which used to annoy me, so I reverted to taking laxatives – many a day. I knew I was becoming hopeless – each time I binged I would be filled with guilt, vowing never to do it again.

'I then saw a notice in the newspaper for a support group. For the past two years I have been attending regularly and have found it a great help.

'I'm still far from better, still bingeing every few weeks, but I have learned to eat relatively normally and can cope with a meal put down in front of me. I have also told my female flatmates, which makes things easier.'

Kate's story

'When I started high school I had a "perfect" figure, then I gradually became aware of it and began my first diet to stay in "shape". But instead of losing weight, this awareness seemed to make me start putting on weight. I went on a diet for six weeks and my weight went down. Then it started up again very quickly.

'About a year later, after a lot of stuffing and throwing up, I started another diet. My weight see-sawed. At eighteen I have gone from near anorexia to stuffing and stuffing, throwing up and using laxatives, but I have still put on a tremendous amount of weight.

31

'Oh God, the suffering and agony, the pressures and depressions. It seems like a never-ending cycle of fast, stuff, throw up, but always putting on weight. Sometimes I cry for help, but where do I go? Who could possibly understand? What happens this time if I forget to stop and end up anorexic or worse? Or what if I start stuffing again and put on weight? I couldn't take it one more time.

'I think the whole problem is far more widespread than anyone imagines. I have two good friends that I went through school with, and both of them have problems with food. One has anorexia and has been having treatment for a year, the other "played around" with stuffing and throwing up and also had massive ups and downs in weight, depending on what was happening in her life at that time.

'Both of them don't know of my secret problem, but they tell me about theirs. I think they would be disappointed to know that I also suffer. Not me, the stable, straight-thinking girl. I don't know what I am, even bulimia seems too narrow a word to describe me.

'So that's me, and two close friends, three out of three. I think of us at primary school, not a care in the world, and look at us now – nervous wrecks.

'I think finally I've had enough – five years of this constant worry, not a day passes without it, a life ruled by food. But God, what's the way out? I'm either on a diet or stuffing, out of control. There's no in-between for me. I haven't had a proper three-meals-a-day for five years. Food is a total obsession, either the lack of or too much. I think finally I've had enough'.

In the rest of the chapter you can begin to explore your own behaviour and feelings around food: it consists mainly of exercises to get you started on a self-help path. This is a good place to start keeping a journal, or notes of your responses to exercises.

We suggest a length of time for each exercise simply as a guide for those who have to plan in advance to have quiet, private time. If a particular exercise brings up a lot of issues for you, spend longer on it, or come back to it. If you find you go through it really quickly it may be that you have thought that particular issue through before. But be aware

It over-powered me

that sometimes we slide quickly through things that are difficult for us.

Some of the exercises (number 8, for example) are ongoing. Do them as often as you find them useful, they may become part of your regular strategy. Always give yourself credit for any small change and be kind to yourself about any lapse. Slow progress in small steps is much more likely to be lasting than any big leap.

If you know someone else who is working through this book, try to arrange a regular time to meet and discuss the ideas and exercises, or even work through some exercises together. Alternatively, a good woman friend may be willing to talk with you regularly. If you have to 'go it alone', give yourself plenty of rewards (a 'pat on the back,' a treat) for trying, for new insights and understandings, and for every step forward.

At every point and with every exercise, you make the decision whether to give up (for now, or for ever) or to go on.

EXERCISE 1: THE BEGINNINGS

Time: 30 minutes, or longer if you really get into writing a lot about your past.

Think about your history of food problems. Write or think about your answers to these questions:

What are your early memories of food?

What was important about it in your childhood family?

What was it linked with – rewards, punishment, celebrations?

At meal times, what behaviour did your family expect?

Did any of this change when you became a teenager? How?

When did food problems first start for you? What age were you?

How did you feel about your body at this time? What body changes were you experiencing?

Where were you living?

What were you doing – school, work, travelling?

What changes were going on for you? What were the most significant events/issues in your life?

Spend some time thinking about your answers. Then consider the relevance of each of the three strands to what you have identified.

We all have a different set of answers to these questions, but one consistent feature for women is the identification of a dieting cycle – fear of being or getting fat, diet, weight loss, weight gains, another diet . . . The starvation of dieting leads to the urge to binge eating which leads to guilt and anxiety, to vomiting and purging, and so another cycle develops. Along with this goes a complex set of emotions that often make us feel bad about ourselves and our bodies, such as 'I'm not a worthwhile person,' 'I'm fat and ugly, why would anyone love me?' All of this is happening in the context of expectations that society has of us as women – that we have a certain 'look' and body size, that we behave in certain ways, that we have certain roles. As we have already said, to deal with our problems of food we need to keep in mind three areas – the social, the emotional and the physical.

34

EXERCISE 2: THE PRESENT

Time: 15 minutes

Write down or think about your answers to these questions:

Is your eating pattern now the same as when your eating problems first started? Is it worse? better? different?

If it is better, can you identify what has changed for you? what you have done that has worked or helped? Remember these as skills and tools that you already have, and can use again.

If it is the same or worse, don't despair. In reading this book you have begun a process of change.

The record-keeping that these exercises ask you to do may increase your tension around food at first. Even if you don't like the information they are giving you, it is the beginning of some control, and so it is worthwhile to persist.

EXERCISE 3: MONITORING – FOOD CHART FOR BINGE-EATERS

Time: 30 minutes the first time, then 10 minutes a day for two weeks.

Often we feel out of control and helpless around food. A useful way to begin regaining control is to keep a chart of what you eat and the circumstances in which you do it for two weeks. It will give you concrete information about your behaviour, what sets you off on a binge – if that is part of your problem – and what keeps the behaviour going. If your problem is more that you *worry* obsessively about what you eat and your body image ('I might get fat') but don't binge, skim through to Exercise 5.

This format is one that has been useful to a lot of women:

○ Set these headings across the top of the longest side of a sheet of paper:

Date	Time	Food/Drinks consumed	Feelings before	Feelings after	Reactions of others

○ Now rule columns which you can proceed to fill in.
○ Identify with a B and a P each time you have binged and/or purged.

○ At the end of each week, identify the number of times you have binged and the number of times you have purged.

It is important to note whether or not you felt physically hungry when you ate, because that helps identify the difference between satisfying physical and emotional hungers. Draw a star by the occasions when you were responding to physical hunger.

Continue working through the book during the two weeks that you are keeping these records. Come back to this section for the following exercise when you have two weeks of records.

EXERCISE 4: AFTER TWO WEEKS

Time: 30 minutes

If bingeing is part of your eating problem, it will be particularly useful to write down your answers to the questions above. They will provide you with a basis for making changes.

Look at your food chart. Can you identify any patterns? Are there particular times when you binge – afternoon? evening? morning? most of the day?

What feelings and pressures are you aware of at this time?

How many times a week do you binge?

How long does the binge last?

What would you be doing with this time if you were not bingeing?

How much time a day or a week does bingeing take?

Are you on your own or with others? who in particular?

What emotions can you identify before you started eating?

How much did you spend on food for bingeing during the two weeks?

If you purged after bingeing:

What methods did you use (vomiting, laxatives, fasting)?

How much time did it take?

How did you feel afterwards?

How much did you spend on laxatives during the two weeks?

List the effects of the bingeing and purging on your physical health.

You will come back to this information as you start planning changes in your behaviour with food. For many, the first step is to stop or reduce purging, otherwise it will always be a 'back-door' for you to escape the consequences of bingeing.

EXERCISE 5: 'IT'S TAKING OVER MY LIFE'

Time: 15 minutes
Draw a pie chart of a typical day in your life. Show how much of the day you spend eating, working, sleeping, etc. If the categories on the sample chart do not apply to your life, create your own.

Sample pie chart for a woman without children:

Total: 24 hours

On your pie chart, shade over the amount of time you spend *thinking* about food.

Feeding many needs

It's understandable that we turn to food at times of emotional need, but it is also important to realize that to ultimately break the cycle and build our self-esteem we need to face the issues underlying the bingeing behaviour, as well as try to change the behaviour.

Food can be used to dull feelings, and help us deal with psychological pain. It has become a coping mechanism for many women. As with alcohol and drugs, eating can be used as a solace, or to blot out negative feelings. Women have used words like 'spacing out', feeling 'nothing', 'in no (wo)man's land' and 'blotted out' to describe the binge/purge experience. It becomes an escape from emotions. 'Time out' is another common phrase that women who binge use.

This is Jackie's description: *'Food plays a major part in my life. I enjoy my food at home or out. It represents a time of pleasure and happiness where often there is company. I think of eating as an enjoyable thing to do – as company and also a comforter. Therefore, if I'm down in the dumps, tired or depressed, eating may be a way of cheering myself up. It gives me something to do if I'm on my own, bored or at a loose end.'*

As women we have strong emotions like anger, loneliness, boredom and frustration (particularly if we are a sexual abuse survivor). The general conditioning of women – often arising from a particular set of family and societal attitudes – is that it's wrong to have strong emotions and that our role is to care for other people, rather than attend to our own feelings. Often our feelings are so suppressed that we are almost unaware that we have them. But they are there, and will make themselves felt in some way – startling outbursts of anger, depression, confusion, low self-esteem, feeling uncomfortable around people or in stress symptoms like heart palpitations, hot and cold flushes, shakiness, aches and pains. This can be frightening and so we learn to fear the feelings. Since we lack role models for the expression of strong feelings, and because we are not supposed to have them, we haven't learnt that they are okay *and* that they can be expressed in constructive ways.

Many of us use our relationship with food as a substitute for actually sharing our emotions with the people involved. We stuff the emotions down with food, or dull them with alcohol and drugs. However, food cannot be treated as a physical addiction; we cannot abstain from it, or even gradually withdraw (as, for example, from minor tranquillizers), because we need it to maintain life. Our relationship with food has become horribly distorted – it is something we love, but at the same time we hate ourselves for 'indulging' in it. And even if we don't binge or purge, we may think of food as a 'solution' to our problems – 'If I don't eat too much much and get/stay thin, my life will improve'. We come to see our relationship with food as the one factor that determines our happiness.

Bingeing and purging can blot out the immediate strong feelings (both negative and positive) but then they create problems of their own – feelings of self-loathing, alienation from other people, losing control, health problems, emotional needs that are not met, high financial cost and a waste of time. The relationship between our feelings and food is discussed in more detail in Chapter 4.

EXERCISE 6: THE GOOD AND THE BAD

Time: 10 minutes
This exercise is to identify the good and bad feelings and thoughts that you get from your particular problem with food.

Example:

GOOD	BAD
I feel in control.	The truth is, I'm not really.
I don't put on weight.	It's damaging my health.
I feel relieved.	I feel trapped in a vicious cycle.

You may also find it helpful to think about the 'friendly' or useful aspects of your particular eating problem. Write down the statement, 'Bulimia (or dieting, or whatever you identify as your eating problem) is my friend.' List what you get out of it and what difficulties it creates for you. Your immediate reaction may be that you can't think of anything that you do get out of it. If so, just keep the idea at the back of your mind for a while. Something may come to the surface later.

Sara is very aware of the rewards and the costs involved in her behaviour with food: *'Bingeing and purging help me to avoid the present moment. (I could be doing more constructive things, i.e. studying, exercising, making friends.) They reinforce negative feelings about myself and serve as a*

*self-punishment, a double-edged sword. For example, I eat
to comfort myself and then feel disgusted at having eaten so
much. I pick up guys to make me feel sexually attractive and
then feel cheap afterwards.'*

It is important to be aware of the rewards that you get
from your particular relationship with food; they are what
keeps the relationship going. Part of the change process for
you will be to challenge and find alternatives for these
rewards, so that your relationship with food can become an
ordinary pleasure.

EXERCISE 7: FOCUSING ON YOURSELF

Time: 30 minutes
What do you visualize when you think about yourself, your
life and your problem with food? What kind of images come
into your mind? Try to draw or write what you can 'see',
perhaps in your journal. Expand the drawing or writing to
include your feelings.

For example, in a group setting, one woman drew a
picture of herself with a huge, heavy weight like a stone on
top of her head. It was a heavy load that she was carrying.
She couldn't see a life beyond because she was so weighed
down by a particular problem. What she wanted to do was
put the weight down, but she didn't know that she could.

Try not to judge yourself for any feelings, images or ideas
that this exercise brings up. Just accept them as giving you
some information about yourself at this moment – 'This is
how I am now.'

EXERCISE 8: FOCUSING ON YOURSELF

Time: 20 minutes
The purpose of this exercise is to gather more information
about yourself and your life.

On a sheet of paper or an empty page in your journal,
draw a symbol for yourself (e.g. a circle or a figure with 'me'
in the middle). Around it draw symbols (circles, squares,
sketches, anything you like) and/or words for the different
aspects of your life: work, family, relationships, sexuality,
friends, leisure-time activities and so on.

How does your problem with food affect each aspect of

your life? Does it affect them all? Shade over the ones that are affected. (Use different coloured pens or densities of shading if you wish.)

Are there things that you are not doing because of your problem with food? Put symbols or words for these on your paper.

Add your dreams and visions of things you would like to be doing.

This exercise will give you information about how your problem with food is working, what or who it is protecting you from. It is not necessary to act immediately on any of the things you become aware of, it is simply helpful to be aware of them at this stage.

Stress

Over ninety per cent of the women in Jasbindar's survey said that they binged when they were under stress. Factors they identified included everyday issues such as problems at work or with relationships, bringing up children, and putting on weight, as well as transitional phases in their lives such as the ending of a relationship, starting a new job, or leaving school. In these circumstances, food was used as a comfort, to relieve the stress. But, as we know, it can also be a cause of stress.

Stress is related to problem-solving, and our perception of the problem. For example, we are inclined to feel stressed when we are faced with a problem we feel we can't deal with. We are often really bad at judging our stress levels. Stress symptoms can include: heart palpitations; hot and cold flushes; pains in the body; fatigue; skin rashes; poor concentration; muscular tension; constipation or diarrhoea; headaches; feelings of being overwhelmed or out of control; continual anxiety that is not about anything specific; feeling 'stressed out' or 'wound up'. It is important to take notice of any of these symptoms if they occur. If you are not a good judge of your own stress levels at first, other people may give you some indication.

Memories and imagination can be a source of stress, particularly for those of us who have violence, sexual abuse, neglect or great loss in our past. It may be necessary to go through the painful process of dealing with our present

41

feelings about those past events: perhaps with professional help.

Worry, which is how we often experience stress, has a useful purpose – it alerts us to the problem, is a trigger for action and enables us to think around the problem. It is no use saying 'Don't worry, there is nothing to worry about', because if you do worry there *is* something there to worry about. Worry can transfer from being a trigger mechanism to a permanent state which makes us feel bad and affects us physically.

Stress is not always a bad thing, because it gives us the push that we often need, and it can be a motivating factor. For most of us, it is hard to imagine a life without stress, but too much of it can tip us over – maybe into a binge. Positive things in our lives can also be stressful – like buying a house or starting a new relationship. Using food is just one way to cope with too much stress, and not necessarily the best way.

So what can you do about stress? Some of the best remedies are very simple, like taking time for rest and relaxation, eating well, exercising regularly, having leisure activities which provide a break, getting enough sleep, finding an alternative to your job and/or domestic chores. The key seems to be having a balance of activities that includes some exercise. Some women find it helpful to make a list of all the things they do and then re-arrange it, crossing some off, asking someone else to do some of them, deciding to stop doing something and so on. For others, identifying and voicing strong feelings (see Chapter 4) may be important.

Try listening to your 'inner voice', that tells you what you need, what you can do to look after yourself. We tend to put such thoughts aside and do what we think we should, giving more weight to what we think than how we feel. When we learn to read them, feelings can be a good source of information for us about what our needs are.

If stress is a big problem for you, particularly if it is a major trigger to bingeing, seek out some of the many books written about it. Public libraries are often well-stocked with books on stress. If you don't relate to the first one you get, try others; there are many approaches and some will suit you more than others.

EXERCISE 9: DAILY BALANCE

Time: 30 minutes.

Draw a pie chart covering twenty-four hours showing how much of your time is spent on various activities – work, social, food, sleep, personal, family, or others that are relevant to your life.

Can you see any changes you can make that would reduce stress? Notice how much time activity with food occupies. How much time of the day do you spend thinking about food?

Are you happy with this pie chart? Is this how you want to spend your day? A lot of women realize how little time they have for themselves when they do this chart. Is this true for you?

In fact, the thought of having spare time can make many women anxious. When food is being used to stuff down feelings, having time that is not filled can be really threatening – it allows those feelings to come to the surface. Keeping busy keeps those feelings at bay, even if it is like running faster and faster on one spot.

Personal time can be for just sitting, or watching TV, or doing anything that you want to do. Is your only personal time when you are with food? How would you like to see personal time on your pie chart?

For many of us, our ideal chart may only be a fantasy because of our social conditions and lack of money – but even then there will be some changes that we can make.

Do you build up your stress level by being constantly busy? For a lot of women whose day is tightly structured, bingeing becomes an escape. For others, keeping busy is a cure or preventative device – it helps them to keep from bingeing. The danger with this is that activity becomes obsessive. Tiredness and low energy levels are things that a lot of women identify as a trigger for a binge.

Does your pie chart look balanced to you? Are there things you can see that you could do to make it more balanced? For example, could you take half an hour here or there to do something you like? Arrange to see friends? Lie in the sun? Take the kids to the beach?

You may find that it makes more sense to look for balance over a few days or a week, rather than one day, but don't make your balance period longer than a week.

EXERCISE 10: PHYSICAL EXERCISE

Time: 15 minutes.

What exercise do you do? (Exercise helps reduce the effect of stress, but not if it is confined to taking the children to school, carrying a load of shopping, or worrying about being late somewhere.) Make a list of your exercise, including things like walking, swimming, jogging, sports, gym, fitness exercises, yoga, aerobics, cycling. Can you make a regular time to do one of these? Walking is one of the best forms of exercise and it's cheap and doesn't require any special equipment. The basic principle for exercise is that it should be regular and use as much of the body as possible.

Stress is a fact of life for most of us. What is important is how we learn to cope with it, reduce or minimize it, and the strategies we learn for coping – are they the best ones for us? Look at your pie chart from Exercise 9. What changes do you need to make to get more exercise?

Premenstrual syndrome (PMS) and stress

'I know it seems like an exaggeration, but it's as though a hungry monster inside me were ready to devour anything sweet, especially chocolate. I'll stuff and stuff myself. Then when I'm finished I suddenly feel calm. I can't believe I lost control again. Sometimes I make myself sick; sometimes I am just depressed and don't bother.'

'I have been a borderline anorexic for years. Before menstruating, though, all I can think about is food. I stare at it, count the calories and imagine eating it. I rarely actually give in to bingeing but it's hard not to.'

Premenstrually, many of us experience cravings, especially for sweet things. This is often triggered by a low blood sugar level at this stage in the cycle: eating sweet things makes it worse. Some other common premenstrual symptoms are: fatigue, headaches, irritability, being more accident prone, being on a short fuse emotionally, depression, anxiety, shakiness, feeling foggy, being unable to think clearly, feeling bloated. Weight fluctuations at this time can be related to fluid retention.

If the days before your period are different from the rest of the month for you, keep a record for about three months of dates and symptoms and see whether there is a pattern or cluster of symptoms that is related to your menstrual cycle. Once you have this information you can use it to look at your activities and how you plan them, making good use of your higher energy times. Tell people around you what is happening (but not if they use it to put you down). Don't use the information to put yourself down, either. The feelings you have with PMS are just as valid as those you have at any other time – the fact that they may be more intense or harder to deal with does not make them any less real. In fact, it is a time when you can get really valuable information for yourself about what your feelings and needs are, and can be a good cleansing period.

For further references about dealing with PMS see Resources.

EXERCISE 11: BREAKING THE RITUAL

Time: 10-15 minutes each time you feel the urge to binge. You may want to start this exercise at the first opportunity or wait until you have been keeping an eating chart for two weeks. It's your decision.
When you feel the urge to binge, take ten to fifteen minutes out and instead of bingeing, change your location. Go to another room or outside and focus on the feelings you are having.

Think about what you could do instead of bingeing.

Write a list of your options. For example, ring a friend – talk about your present feelings if you wish, or about anything at all. Don't ring anyone who is likely to make you feel bad or activate the sorts of feelings that lead you to binge.

Identify any activities or strategies or rituals or spaces that make you feel okay. (Have a bath, massage, read, walk around the garden, play with the cat/dog/children, play your favourite music, invite your partner to make love, wallow in bed, masturbate, fantasize about winning a lottery, do patchwork, knitting, some free expression with crayons/ paints/felts . . .)

If after the fifteen minutes has passed the urge to binge is still there, do it – you make the choice.

If you have binged, then go through the same process to decide whether or not you will purge.

Distracting yourself from the feelings of discomfort and fullness by going for a walk, visiting or ringing a friend – whatever is a suitable distraction for you – may help you avoid purging.

It is known that stopping the purging leads to less bingeing. You will probably have to deal with anxiety about putting on weight (Re-read the Fat Phobia section in Chapter 1. Body image is dealt with in detail in Chapter 5.) We have found that with normal eating habits a woman's weight will adjust to what is appropriate for her body. This may be a few more kilos than your ideal, but is unlikely to reach anything near your worst fears.

EXERCISE II: BREAKING THE WEIGHING RITUAL

Time: a few minutes

What sort of relationship do you have with your scales? How many times a day/week do you weigh yourself? How do you feel when your weight is up? When it is down? Do you weigh yourself on different scales at every opportunity you get?

If you are weighing yourself more than once a month, the focus on your weight is probably reinforcing your problem with food. If you don't want to give your scales away, reduce the number of times you weigh yourself to no more than once a day, then every other day and so on. You decide how often. The purpose is to reduce the importance that you give to what you weigh. It can be quite liberating to not know your weight to the last gram.

3 Food for Thought

Anne: *'I would like to eat sensible meals and be a normal eater but I can't see it happening.'*

Betty: *'Before I knew it, I didn't know how to eat sensibly, and so had the "all or nothing" attitude.'*

April (mother): *'She says she can stop being sick any time, but I feel she now has no control over it at all. She won't eat any regular meals and if she does, she brings it up within half an hour.'*

Pauline: *'I seem to have lost sight of how much food is a "normal" intake, which does worry me. (Another loss of control.) I realize the serious health implications, but the thought of giving it up makes me feel panicky. I have been making a real effort lately but the thought of sitting down to a real meal without recourse to getting rid of it is frightening.'*

Christine: *'My eating habits are very irregular. I go for days without eating, just having cups of black coffee, then I'll go on a binge, feeling totally bloated and ill afterwards. Then, feeling ill, I won't eat again for a while, then back to the bingeing. At times I can eat a normal evening meal if I'm eating at someone's house, but more often than not, I just don't feel as if I can eat at all. Often I can't bring myself to vomit after eating and just sleep it off.'*

Shona: *'As soon as I get "down" or have gone what I consider to be slightly overboard, I binge. For example a meal out the other night triggered a binge – I had chips with the main course when I hadn't intended to.'*

Problems with food cannot be dealt with by ignoring them or 'giving up' food, because we need food for survival. But we have often learnt that even the slightest 'indulgence' in food is bad for us – we will become fat and ugly and no longer be sexy, acceptable or desirable.

47

Current diets and pressure to be thin encourage us to deprive ourselves of food. As a result, we feel hungry and have thoughts about 'denying ourselves'. This denial can stop us eating – for a while – but it usually doesn't stop us thinking about food.

The fear of getting fat distorts our attitudes towards food and eating and so we come to see food as an enemy – we deny it to our bodies and it seems to take over our minds. This combination of hunger and obsessive thinking about food often leads to a binge. To change this, it is important that we think long-term, revising our attitudes towards food and our eating patterns, rather than taking the short-term approach 'I must lose weight now.' We need to develop healthy and pleasurable responses to food.

Counting calories or depriving our bodies of food are simply inappropriate. There is plenty of evidence that dieting, which to our bodies means starvation, actually creates the urge to binge. We believe that the best and healthiest relationship with food is based, not on denial, but on 'common-sense' ideas about healthy eating.

For long-term sound functioning and good health, we need to eat all types of food regularly and in reasonable proportions – the old idea of a 'balanced diet' is a good one.

There's something very basic about being able to sustain our bodies. How can we have a healthy relationship with things around us when we don't have a healthy relationship with our own body, and when we are constantly denying our basic need for proper nutrition? The side-effects of eating *can* be good health and the enjoyment of food. How we feel about ourselves affects our relationships with the people around us. The old saying 'To love others you must first love yourself' is very true – and an important aspect of loving ourselves is to give ourselves food that is nutritious and enjoyable.

Food Facts

Every year there are 'new' healthy eating ideas promoted by all sorts of people. Many weight-loss diets are promoted as containing all the nutrients we need to be healthy, like the 'scientifically prepared drink containing all the proteins, vitamins, minerals and trace elements you need . . .' A drink three times a day does not meet anyone's need for food. Cautioning people against very low calorie diets, *Consumer* magazine (May 1988) commented, 'you could deprive your body of enough energy to maintain good health'.

As with everything, there are fads and fashions around food, but the basic idea of 'balanced nutrition' looks set to last. A very broad guide for healthy eating would be:

○ Eat a variety of foods.
○ Eat for nutrition *and* pleasure, not to regulate your body size.
○ Don't eat too much sugar, fat or salt.

Basically, if you eat some of all the main food groups every day – fresh fruit, vegetables (the fresher the better), protein (chicken, fish, meat, tofu, or other soya bean products, nuts), carbohydrates (cereals, bread, rice, etc) – you will have a healthy diet. Health Department publications usually include milk products as one of the food groups, but for many people there are allergy problems associated with them. However, they are a source of protein and calcium, so if you *are* avoiding milk products, make sure you are getting these from other sources.

EXERCISE 1: HOW DO I THINK ABOUT FOOD?

Time: 15 minutes
Spend about five minutes writing or thinking about your attitudes to food, then consider these questions:

Do you have conflicting ideas and feelings about food? For example, I really love to eat, but it's something I shouldn't allow myself to do.

Are most of your attitudes negative ('Food is bad for me, it makes me fat') or positive ('I love to go out to dinner')?

Do you think your attitudes are realistic? Can you live a satisfactory, healthy life with the attitudes you have?

EXERCISE 2: HOW CAN I START TO THINK POSITIVELY ABOUT FOOD?

Time: 20 minutes
A. For five minutes write, in a column on one side of a

page, all the negative things you think about food in relation to yourself.

Now write a positive version of every statement alongside it. For example:

Negative	Positive
Food makes me fat.	Food is good for me it gives me energy and vigour.
Eating takes control of me.	I can enjoy eating and stop when I want to.
Eating is disgusting.	Eating is natural.

You may not believe these positive statements but doing this exercise can be a start to changing the way you think about food. Whenever you have a negative thought about food, start trying to turn it into a positive. That way you will become aware of the possibility of different ways of thinking, even if you don't believe the positives right now.

B. Write the following statements in your journal or on something that you can pin on the wall so that you see them often.[8]

1. *Occasional binge eating is normal eating behaviour*
2. *Following food restriction with significant weight loss, all human beings become preoccupied with food. When food is freely available again, a proportion of people binge-eat for months.*
3. *There are no intrinsically unhealthy foods – it is all a matter of degree of intake.*
4. *Average daily intake of food fluctuates between 1500 and 3000 calories, depending on energy output, social stimuli, and emotional and physical state.*
5. *Anything 'forbidden' or 'not allowed' becomes over-valued.*

As you write these statements, think about what they mean for you.

From our experience, the most successful approach to changing your eating behaviour will be to set up a regular eating pattern – say three or four meals a day at more or less regular times.

Remember, you are not planning yet another weight-control diet, you are planning to regain a 'normal' eating pattern. Allow for snack times (morning and afternoon tea) as well if you wish. Try to be reasonable rather than rigid.

It may be really difficult at first to allow yourself to eat this way because of your fear of getting fat. Try putting this on hold – you may gain a few kilos but once you establish a healthy eating pattern in response to your body's needs, your weight will stabilize at what is normal for you, although this may be more than you think is ideal (see the information and discussion about 'set points', p. 19).

EXERCISE 3: SETTING A REGULAR EATING PATTERN

Time: 30 minutes

Take a new page in your journal or a sheet of paper. Divide it into sections that relate to the way an ordinary day is for you.

Sample:
Get up 8 a.m.
Get to work 9.00
Tea break 10.15
Lunch 12.30
Afternoon tea break 3.15
Home from work 5.30
Evening
(Yours may be quite different from this.)

Refer back to the information you gathered in Exercise 3 and 4 in Chapter 2. This will help you to plan your eating times so that you have eaten at least one, and maybe two or three times *before* you come to your usual bingeing time.

Choose three or four times during the day when you will eat something. Make one of the times between getting up and going to work. To begin with it doesn't matter if you eat only a very little at some of your eating times, but do eat something. If you have a pattern of not eating early in the day and feel that you are never hungry at this time, start really small and don't restrict yourself to traditional breakfast foods. Have something you really like.

Select your own foods for your other eating times.

51

The important point in this exercise is to establish *regular* eating. Once you have established your eating times, try not to think too much about what you will eat, just do it. For some women writing down a week's programme in detail is helpful; for others, it is better to be more spontaneous. The choice is yours.

What you eat at each time is completely up to you. It will help a lot if you can have some control over food preparation where you live. If your flatmate or parents cook food you hate, see if you can negotiate some changes. If you are a mother with young children, think about how food preparation is organized in your household and see if you can set up a system with your partner that will enable you to eat what you want to eat when you want to eat it.

Set up a separate routine for weekend and holidays if your activities have a different structure then.

You may need help to set up this programme if your eating has become really distorted – ask a friend who you think is fairly well informed about food or a dietitian to help you. The point is to get in touch with what your body needs, so that you can learn to eat when you are hungry and stop eating when you are full. If you cannot recognize your body's basic signals, this structure will help you to get back in touch. If you are in the habit of skipping meals, it's important to establish a pattern of eating regularly, at least three times a day.

If you have had problems with eating for a long time, don't expect to establish this pattern easily. Congratulate yourself for any success ('Wow! I actually ate something before I left for work this morning') and try not to make a crisis out of any lapses, like not eating breakfast. If you do skip eating first thing, you *haven't* ruined the day, you can decide to eat something at your next break or whenever. You are not likely to achieve a 'perfect' routine straight away as your mind and body have been in a state of confusion about food for some time.

EXERCISE 4: FOOD IS MY FRIEND

Time: 20 minutes the first time you do it, then less.
Write *'Food is my friend'*
Then write all the negative things that come into your mind.

52

Set it out like this:

Food is my friend
It is not, it's my enemy. (These are sample answers. Write your own responses).
Food is my friend
It can't be, I hate it and I'm sick of thinking about it.
Food is my friend
Rubbish, it makes me fat.
Food is my friend
Well, I certainly can stuff myself.
Food is my friend
Well I suppose it keeps me going.

Keep going like this until you can't think of any more negative things to say about food. Write the phrase one last time and follow it with a positive statement (it may be hard the first time). For example:

Food is my friend
Well, I certainly like to eat.

Do this exercise every day for a week or two, or for as long as you feel you are getting something out of it. After repeating it a number of times you may be able to write '*Food is my friend*' and 'Yes, I can eat according to what my body needs – and enjoy it.'

Changing our eating habits is a difficult process – always reward yourself for any successes and be forgiving about lapses. If you eat a bar of chocolate before your period or when under stress you haven't 'blown' everything, you've just eaten a bar of chocolate. Instead, remember each moment is a moment of choice – you can start afresh. Plan your next meal, making it really enjoyable and nourishing. Include at least one 'treat'.

EXERCISE 5: CHANGING THOUGHT PATTERNS

Time: 15 minutes the first time, then a few minutes each time it comes up.
This exercise can help you change the thought processes that lead from eating a bar of chocolate (or a doughnut, or whatever) to a full scale binge on the 'If-I'm-not-perfect-then-I'm-the-pits' scale of thinking. Begin with your usual reaction:

First Phase: 'I've eaten a bar of chocolate (or whatever). The whole day is down the tubes, it's going to be a bad day, I've ruined everything. I'm on to a binge.'
(Sample) And deliberately change it:
Second phase: 'Hang on a minute. How can a bar of chocolate ruin a whole day? (Keep challenging yourself.) Do I have to binge just because I've eaten a bar of chocolate? I can still do . . . and . . . today, and maybe I'll go for a run or a swim later if I feel like it. That was a yummy bar of chocolate. Now what is it that I have to do next? (Take a walk, a bath, call a friend, or some other distraction.)

The purpose of this exercise is for you to keep challenging the thoughts that lead you into a major eating binge because you ate something 'naughty'. It is to get away from the attitude that if you are not perfect (you ate the chocolate), then you must be an absolute failure so you might as well binge.

Again, remember to give yourself credit for any success or change – I managed not to binge at lunchtime, I'm learning new skills – and that change is usually difficult and slow. If you try the thought-challenging process and do go on to binge, don't berate yourself as a total failure, tell yourself, 'Oh well, it didn't work this time, but I'll keep trying.' (If you are still having problems with purging after a binge, refer back to Exercise 11 in Chapter 2.)

As you establish a healthy eating pattern, you will feel more in touch with sensations of taste and hunger, and what you feel like eating. It's a gradual process. Keep congratulating yourself every time you eat an ordinary meal or have a period without bingeing or purging, and forgive yourself for lapses.

Get into the habit of not going hungry. If you take laxatives, plan to gradually replace them with fresh fruit and wholegrain foods. (If you have been a heavy laxative user, your bowel may not immediately function normally. Get medical advice if you experience any problems.)

Think about the people you live with and whether you want to tell them what you are doing. It helps if you can talk with and get support from those around you, but if you think they won't be supportive, find a friend who will encourage you when you are going through a bad patch and reinforce your successes. It can be very difficult to get support if you are isolated (including being with a partner or flatmate who is uncommunicative or not understanding), if you have poor health or young children, or are living on your own in a new place. Keeping a journal, as we suggested earlier, can be particularly valuable if you are in one of these situations.

EXERCISE 6: MEETING UNMET NEEDS Time: 15 minutes

For some of us, food is the only positive, rewarding thing in our life. For example, we may be living in a new town without family or friends, in a relationship that is no longer as nurturing as it used to be, or we don't feel confident around other people. So we eat for comfort, believing that food is our only friend. Breaking out of this eating cycle to set up new eating patterns will seem very difficult and you may ask, 'where do I start?'

adds to an already low self-esteem

guilt/failure,
feelings of self-pity

lack of positive
experiences in your life

bingeing/using food for comfort

The aim of this exercise is to break the cycle illustrated in the diagram.

Write a list of the needs you have that you feel are not being met. (This list is just for you, don't worry about hurting anyone else's feelings.)

Once you have identified these needs, think about a step you can take to change each situation. Make it a small step, like asking a friend for a cuddle, rather than a big one, like finding a loving relationship within a month. Set out to realize as many of the steps you have identified as you can.

Don't despair if you feel right now that your needs can't be met. Later chapters will deal with these issues in more detail. Once a more regular eating pattern has been established it becomes easier to heed the messages our body gives us, like craving fresh fruit and vegetables after a few days without them.

Or we might fancy a doughnut and be able to have one without turning it into a binge. (Those of us who have been on a bingeing cycle may find that it takes a long time to achieve this. There is no set time frame, it may take anything from weeks to months. Any lessening of purging or bingeing is progress.) Food *can* become one of the pleasures of our lives, it can be sensuous and friendly.

Once a more regular eating pattern has been established it becomes easier to heed the messages our body gives us, like craving fresh fruit and vegetables after a few days without them. Or we might fancy a doughnut and be able to have one without it turning into a binge. (Those of us who have been in a bingeing cycle may find that it takes a long time to achieve this. There is no set time frame, it may take anything from weeks to months. Any lessening of purging or bingeing is progress.) Food *can* become one of the pleasures of our lives, it can be sensuous and friendly.

4 Coping with Feelings

Heather's Story

'I've had bulimia and I'm not "cured" yet, but am a lot better
than I was. I started vomiting two and a half years ago. The
first time was when I ate too much because I knew I had to
cope alone yet again getting two young kids off to bed. My
husband was at the pub – Friday night – my son always
seemed colicky around this time and my daughter would
perform to get my attention when she was tired. I had eaten
and eaten in the afternoon and felt awful. I remembered my
sister telling me a friend of hers used to make herself sick, so
I thought I'd try it.

'I can't remember much about the next year, except that I
was vomiting at least once a week. I talked my husband into
shifting jobs and leaving the small town we were living in. (I
would have left him otherwise.) All he seemed to be doing
was boozing, spending money and socializing in the off-
season and getting uptight and depressed when he was
working.

'The shift helped, but my eating problem continued. I had
a kind of unconscious drive to be sick every sixth day at
least. I started a diary and this was the biggest help of all for
me – it helped me to see that it wasn't my fault when I got
depressed. There were outside reasons. I still felt shut in with
two pre-schoolers and had little money, and I hated the
school holidays, when the creche used to close – it was my
weekly treat to leave my older daughter there and my son
asleep in the backpack for a couple of hours. I read a lot of
feminist books and bought some on bulimia. I tried the Fat
is a Feminist Issue way of eating but found it too much
pressure, writing down everything I ate, and I was too far
from shops to get what I felt like.

'We shifted again a year later. I remember it because I was
being sick every day. My husband didn't like his boss and
there were lots of interviews for new jobs, some just missing
out. There was a lot of pressure.

'I went to a naturopath a few months after we shifted. I thought it might all be related to food allergies, having read about them. Usually on a binge I eat lots of white bread with honey or golden syrup. I got piles of tablets, a special diet. I stuck at it for three weeks, vomited and slowly gave it all up. I told my husband about the bulimia – I had to explain the money for the naturopath, I sometimes wish I hadn't, as all it did was make him pressure me more at mealtimes to eat and a couple of times he's called me a "nut-case" when he was angry – which really hurt.

'I tried recording my eating again, and having what I wanted. I think it helped – I lived on cheese and sultanas. My daughter went to school at the start of this year and I just have my son at home. I don't want any more children and sometimes am afraid in case I accidentally get pregnant.

'I found out my younger sister is also bulimic. She is obsessed with being thin and uses food as an escape from pressure. She is a perfectionist.

'I went to a few support group meetings but haven't been for a while. It's good to know the group is there in case I backslide.

'This year I'm doing a university paper and a class at the local high school – they have a creche there. I bought a second-hand typewriter recently and am learning to type. I used to do spinning before, but I need intellectual stimulation as well.

'I haven't vomited for about three to four weeks. The last bad time was Christmas but I managed to regain control. I have only been vomiting about once a month since February. I still over-eat when I am depressed, anxious, or alone, but not by the same amount and I seem to know I have control.'

By now you will have identified that there is a strong connection between our feelings about ourselves and our attitudes and responses to food. You may have experienced compulsive eating in response to a feeling or a muddle of confused feelings. Sally wrote, 'A large part of my eating is related to stuffing feelings down my throat, and not feeling nourished in emotional ways.'

Feelings that women have identified as being associated with bingeing are: anger, loneliness, boredom, frustration, anxiety, depression, tiredness, confusion and uncertainty, being upset, insecurity and even feeling happy or excited. This suggests that binge eating can be a response to intense emotions. Also, in relation to our problems with food, we know that the emptier we feel emotionally, the more likely we are to fill the gaps with food.

Psychologist Albert Ellis (1962) originated an ABC model of human behaviour called the Rational Emotive Theory (RET). This theory demonstrates the relationship between thinking, feeling and behaviour. Simply put, A stands for activity or situation, B for belief, thinking or attitudes, and C for consequences, which are feelings. In relation to someone with a problem with food:

A = an activity or situation, such as eating a chocolate bar.

B = the person starting to believe irrationally that, because they have eaten a chocolate bar, 'I've destroyed my whole day. I have no control over my eating and my life, I'm a total failure and that's just unbearable.'

C = the person consequently feeling depressed, self-loathing, fat, anxious and worthless.

So, according to the theory, our feelings are determined by our thoughts in a particular situation. Ellis suggested extending the theory to points D and E, so at point D the irrational beliefs are disputed and challenged. For example, 'So what if I ate more than I wanted, I actually enjoyed the taste. It's not true I have no control, I have not binged for xx amount of time and that is progress for me.' At point E more rational ideas are substituted for the irrational beliefs that were expressed previously. For example, 'I feel uncomfortable having binged, but in future I will be more careful not to "set the stage" for bingeing by starving myself.' Or, another example of E: 'I have not destroyed my whole day and I can still have a healthy meal at dinner time.'

Our emotional reactions grow out of the ways we see ourselves. According to Ellis, a change in unhealthy emotional patterns can come only with a change in our thinking or our perception of reality. So our feelings are a reflection of our deeper attitudes. While it is important to acknowledge and deal with these feelings, we also need to develop different attitudes towards food, weight and our body image.

Bingeing can be a response to starvation brought on by a

weight-loss diet (ninety per cent of the women in Jasbindar's survey started their bulimia by dieting), or by not allowing yourself to eat breakfast or lunch. But, in the long term, bingeing is punishing yourself and your body. It denies the underlying causes of and the strong feelings you may have, especially given our conditioning as women to believe that strong feelings are bad and shouldn't be expressed.

Whatever feelings you have are valid – they are telling you something about your interactions with the people around you and the world in general. They are not good or bad in themselves, they are simply feelings. The crucial thing is what we do with them.

EXERCISE 1: IDENTIFYING FEELINGS

Time: 30 minutes.

Think about the last time you had a strong emotion, felt that there was something amiss, experienced a nagging dissatisfaction, confusion or something similar. (You may like to write your thoughts about these in your journal.) If you can't identify any strong feeling, try to remember the last time you said 'I don't mind' or 'It doesn't really matter', cried or felt like crying, and work from there.

If you feel really blocked about identifying feelings, try making contact with nature by watching the sky, going to the beach, or taking a walk amongst trees. For many women, this gets you in touch with yourself and your feelings. Alternatively, try watching a sad movie, doing some art work (painting, drawing) or another form of creative self-expression. Another possibility is to work to the end of this chapter and then come back to the exercise.

What was the feeling you found yourself thinking about? Try to name it quite specifically; rather than 'I felt bad', identify the actual feelings: 'I felt angry and resentful when . . .' or 'I felt hurt when . . .' and so on. It takes practice to get in touch with what our feelings are. Just keep trying to identify them very specifically and expect to be confused about them at first.

Think about what you did with the feelings. Did you cry, distract yourself by doing something, talk to a friend, binge, shout at someone, put yourself down and say negative things about yourself in your head? Write them down in as much detail as you can. Don't judge yourself – just note that you had a binge, cried or whatever. Don't punish yourself for it.

Doing the exercise might stimulate some strong feelings. See this as positive and make use of it. What are they telling you? Feelings can seem overwhelming and frightening, so remember that actually *having* them never killed anyone. You may feel that if you start crying, you will cry for ever, but it *will* come to an end! If you can, set up some support for yourself; talk with other women – or the person closest to you – it will help.

EXERCISE 2: IDENTIFYING AND OWNING FEELINGS

Time: 20 minutes.
Write: *I have a right to have my feelings.*

Write your negative reaction, e.g.: *No I don't, they just cause trouble.*

Write it again: *I have a right to have my feelings.*

Negative reaction, e.g.: *But I feel guilty having them.*

Write it again: *I have a right to have my feelings.*

Negative reaction, e.g.: *Lots of people are worse off than me, I shouldn't feel bad.*

Keep writing the statement and your negative reaction until you can't think of any more. Finish by writing the original statement really big and bold. (You may not really believe it the first time you do the exercise, but write it anyway.) Repeat the exercise from time to time until you can write positive statements (e.g. *I certainly do!*) after you have written *I have a right to have my feelings.*

Use the same process with the statement, *I have a right to acknowledge my feelings and deal with them in an appropriate way.*

Some examples of negatives that come up are: *But if I get angry no one will like me, I might lose control, the feelings will go on for ever,* or *I might not be able to express my feelings so that I am understood,* and so on.

As we have said, whatever feelings we have are valid. They give us information about how we are reacting to the world and what we want. The more we deny our feelings, the more they stay with us in some shape or form, and the more persistent they will be. Often we do not recognize this process in our attempts to block feelings with food, alcohol or whatever other means we may use.

Dealing with feelings

There are three main ways we deal with feelings: we express, repress or suppress them.

Expressing feelings can help you 'get things off your chest', 'clear the air', and be close to people. Appropriate ways of expressing feelings are looked at later in this chapter.

Repressed feelings are feelings denied and turned inwards on ourselves. The results can be physical symptoms such as headaches, stomach pains, skin rashes, constant tiredness and sleep disturbance. Many illnesses such as high blood pressure, stomach ulcers, asthma, migraine and depression can be associated with repressed feelings.

Feelings may be suppressed because it is inappropriate to express them at a particular time. However, there is a danger that they will then become repressed. They need to be dealt with later, as they will not just disappear.

As women, some of us have learnt that we shouldn't want things for ourselves. Our role is to care for everyone else, so we develop ways of repressing and not taking notice of our feelings. We do what others expect of us, and don't have any space for noticing the information our feelings give us. For example, your supervisor at work may make suggestive comments about your body, but because he's otherwise friendly and helpful you think you shouldn't mind and try to put up with it. Actually, you're angry (and rightly so as it's sexual harassment) but as you feel you can't express that anger (it doesn't seem appropriate), you pretend it's not there.

Another example: You feel crowded, as though you never have time for yourself, you are kept so busy caring for your partner and children. You talk to your partner about it and he says 'Fair enough' and takes the kids out for the afternoon. As soon as they have gone, you feel miserable and lonely at home by yourself and wish you'd gone with them. You have identified one lot of feelings (feeling overwhelmed as a consequence of too many demands on you), but when your request is met, you are disappointed. This is hardly surprising, as you have not had a lot of practice at being by yourself. Maybe next time you can plan ahead, deciding what you will do while your partner and children are away. Or you may plan to go out on your own. Your second lot of feelings (loneliness, disappointment) have given you more information about what you want.

An example to do with food: You have told your partner or flatmate or friend that you are having problems with food and the next time you are having dinner they ask 'Should you be having that second helping?' You feel guilty and don't have it. But underneath you may feel resentful that someone is trying to control your eating for you. You want to say so but you don't know how to and anyway you don't feel entitled to because it has been said 'for your own good'.

Being assertive

Learning to share and communicate our feelings takes courage and practice. The way we express our feelings affects the people around us and how they react to us, which in turn affects whether or not we get our message across. Once we are more able to identify our feelings, we are more able to express them.

If we can express our feelings assertively, we are more likely to do so in an appropriate way and so give a clear message. There are three aspects to assertive communication:

1. It is direct and says 'I am angry', rather than crashing the dishes and hoping that someone will notice, or swallowing the anger with a binge.

2. It says what we are feeling rather than accusing the other person: 'I'm angry that you . . .' rather than 'You make me mad'.

3. Any situation is dealt with immediately if appropriate, or acknowledged so that we can bring it up later.

Being assertive is very different from being aggressive. Aggressive behaviour is people forcing their ideas or will on to others: coercing them emotionally or physically. Assertive behaviour is simply giving your 'messages' directly and clearly. A person with good self-esteem is able to be assertive without aggression, and be humble without being passive.

Part of being assertive is believing we have a right to express our needs and feelings – a really big hurdle for many of us – instead of worrying about how people will respond to them: 'If I say how I feel, people will think I'm selfish' and 'If I get angry I'll look ugly'.

Once you've identified a feeling, it is useful to think about what it is telling you, what information you can get from it. For example, if you start with the realization that 'I don't like my boss constantly referring to my body', then you can start thinking about what action to take. Or if a man you know has a habit of pinching your bottom, commenting on your weight, and comparing your body with other women's, you can identify what that makes you feel and then decide whether or not, or how you will act. You can decide whether you want to say 'That's offensive', 'Don't do that!' or whatever.

When we are beginning to be assertive, we often undermine our words with our body language – like looking at the floor and avoiding eye contact when we're asking for something, or giggling at the end of a statement, like 'I want to know in advance when you won't be in for dinner'. This doesn't help our statements to be taken seriously.

Being assertive may not always lead to a desired outcome; it won't always make someone else do what they don't want to. However, regardless of the outcome of a particular incident, we feel better about ourselves if we know that we made our point of view clear. We have been able to affirm our sense of self-worth.

There are a number of books that deal with assertiveness (see Resources).

EXERCISE 3: DEALING WITH CRITICISM FROM OTHERS

Time: 10 minutes for the practice, a few seconds when it occurs.
Think back to a time when you were criticised. What was the criticism?

Example: Your flatmate/mother/partner said, 'Should you be eating that?'

What did you think/feel?

Example: 'I've got no privacy, I can't even decide for myself what to eat. But maybe I shouldn't be eating it, anyway . . .'

What did you say and do?

Example: Said nothing, ate it and felt guilty, judged, and resentful?

What could you have said and done?

Example: 'I will decide what and when I eat. I will eat that because I want to.'

The point here is for *you* to decide how valid the criticism is and how much notice to take of it – you evaluate the criticism and respond accordingly.

There are some particular sorts of criticism that it is useful to be aware of:

A. The global, where you are accused of *always* doing something. For example, 'You are always late.' Respond by deciding whether or not it's true: 'I'm sorry, I am late today but I'm usually on time.' If it is true, decide whether you are going to do anything about it: 'Yes, I am often late. We'd better allow more time for me to get here in future.'

B. The total judgement of you as a person, for example, 'You are a very pushy woman.' Again, you decide how much to accept: 'I certainly am working hard to get this creche going because I believe it's really important, but I don't generally think of myself as "pushy".' Or, 'Our relationship would be fine if you didn't have problems with food.' Your decision: 'Yes, I agree that it does have an effect, but there are two of us involved, and *we* need to sort out our relationship'.

C. The comment that is unclear – you don't know whether it is a judgement or not: 'You're seeing a counsellor. How interesting.' So you wonder whether the friend who said it somehow thinks less of you because you are. The only way to deal with this situation is to get more information. 'What do you mean by "interesting?" '

D. The value judgement – what's right for me will be right for you. For example, 'You should try this marvellous diet, I've lost xx kilos.' Try being really direct: e.g. 'I'm trying to establish a regular eating pattern at the moment and not going on diets.'

The criticisms that are implied in stereotypes are ones that we easily internalize. They can work very subtly but powerfully, controlling the thoughts and feelings we have about ourselves. A lot of our feelings of inadequacy arise when we do not match stereotypes.

The media play a major role in promoting and reinforcing sex role stereotypes by:
O failing to represent women in their full variety of ages, sizes and colours;
O failing to reflect the increasing diversity of women's lives;
O failing to portray a representative range of occupations that women hold;
O maintaining the invisibility of women in discussions on many issues;
O portraying women as sexual lures and decorative objects;
O maintaining the invisibility of female experts and decision-makers;
O using language which assumes everyone is male unless identified otherwise.[9]

Psychologist Sue Fitchett says that both the internalization of stereotypical roles (perfect daughter/mother/wife/caregiver/career woman, etc.) and the prohibitions taught in cultures and families, lead to what she calls 'negative self-talk'. She suggests the following exercise to help change this.

EXERCISE 4: TOWARDS MORE POSITIVE · THOUGHTS ABOUT OURSELVES

Time: 20 minutes or more, depending on monitoring time, as often as you choose to do it.
Monitor the statements about yourself that you make in your head ('self-talk') over a period of time – e.g. from getting up until when you leave home in the morning, while the baby is asleep, travelling to or from a destination. If

possible, keep a written record – in your journal if you are keeping one.

Identify which self-talk is;
○ Tentative
○ Clobbering ('I have never been able to control my problems with food. I'm hopeless!')
○ 'Catastrophizing' ('I can't say anything to my mother about the way she pressures me to eat or she'll stop caring about me.')
○ Positive ('I haven't binged for three days – it's been hard but I'm really pleased with myself.')

Practice 'thought-stopping' negatives; when you identify a negative thought, say to yourself (out loud at first if you are on your own, otherwise silently) '*Stop!*' and insert a positive thought instead. For example, you may be starting to think badly about yourself because you binged at lunchtime. Say '*Stop!*' and think something positive: 'I didn't vomit afterwards, that's great' or 'It's my first binge for three days, that's real progress.'

To begin with, do this exercise for a selected time period (say, an hour) and gradually extend the time so the negative self-talk fades out.

Dealing with anger

Anger is a difficult emotion for many of us to deal with. We have learned that it is not appropriate for women to be angry. But as Sheila Ernst and Lucy Goodison say in *In Our Own Hands,*

'. . . you cannot banish feelings by condemning them as "nasty" or "incorrect", any more than you can banish them by reassurance. Difficult or irrational feelings don't go away by being censored, denied or avoided; they go away by being recognized and worked through. What we feel is largely determined by our upbringing, conditioning and our position as women in society which make it, for example, very hard for any woman to be unaware of her appearance. We will stop being affected by such feelings only by exploring them, tracing their origins, and getting them out of our system through expressing them. Then the work of slowly building new structures and ways of relating can be done on a solid basis of feeling, not of guilt and "shoulds" . . .

'. . . It is not considered acceptable for a woman to express her anger in our society. With many pressures on us, and no outlets for our anger, we often end up turning this anger against ourselves. This frequently takes the form of depression or self-hatred. It is important for us to learn to accept our anger and to direct it outwards where it belongs.'

Everyone feels angry sometimes – different things trigger it off. It is better not to let it smoulder away inside or explode like a volcano.

Steps to deal with anger

1. Get in touch with it by owning it ('I am angry') instead of denying, avoiding, suppressing. Try to identify the emotions behind it (see Exercises 1 and 2 in this chapter).

2. Express your anger. Let off steam by physical means, e.g. go for a run, hit a punching-bag, punch cushions; or verbally, e.g. shout in the car, talk to a person concerned directly; or by writing, which you may choose to send or not.

3. Identify unfinished anger. This could include childhood hurts, feelings towards parents, or rejection from a broken relationship. Deal with the anger by writing letters (to send or not), directly with the person(s) concerned, or by talking about it with somebody you trust.

4. Learn some anger management skills:
   ○ Deal with issues while they are still small.
     Take time out.
   ○ Express anger using 'I' statements rather than 'You' ('make me angry').
   ○ Deal with it early and at the source.
   ○ Take responsibility – you have a choice about what you do with your anger.
   ○ Work on your relationship to develop communication.

It is useful to distinguish between personal anger at the people we know and care about, and the anger we feel when we see the injustices of the world. For instance, when a friend doesn't get a job because she's a lesbian, a child gets molested, you read the figures about the average pay rates for women being seventy-four per cent of men's, you can't

68

get a flat because of your skin colour, you keep seeing examples of people being discriminated against because they have a disability, your anger can lead to getting involved in action for a change.

EXERCISE 5: ANGER

Time: 20 minutes
Write or think about answers to these questions:
○ When was the last time you felt angry?
○ Did you express it?
○ How?
○ What effect did it have?
○ If you didn't express it, what stopped you?
○ Was it a fear of consequences? (If I say something he'll walk out or hit me.)
○ Or was it internalized messages? (I really shouldn't express how I feel . . . Mothers aren't supposed to have feelings . . . I get confused . . . Nothing ever changes anyway . . . Peace at any cost . . . I'm not going to be a screaming shrew like my mother . . .
○ Did you deal with your anger by bingeing?

Think back to what triggered your angry feelings.

Re-run what happened in your mind, with you doing nothing but describing how you're feeling (I am angry about . . .), and then saying what you wanted changed (In future, I would like . . .).

Imagine the outcome. (Remember it may not be any different, particularly if the other person is uncooperative or hostile.)

Write down some of the things you would like to be able to say in situations where you get angry or want someone to change their behaviour. Practice saying them with a friend or out loud to a mirror. When you try it in a real-life situation, you may not change the other person's behaviour, but you will have given your message clearly and made your feelings known. Congratulate yourself for trying.

The people around us are used to us as we are. Any change in our behaviour will disturb them and they will do all sorts of things to make us go back to the way we were.

69

('Are you turning into one of those aggressive feminists or something?', 'What's wrong with you? You've become so negative', 'You're never satisfied these days, what more do you want?' or 'You used to be nice.')

In order to deal with what is making you angry, you will be wanting other people to change and they will probably resist this. This will give you a whole new set of feelings to deal with. You may also be forced to make decisions about changes in your life.

Remember not to give yourself a hard time for being unable to express anger right now. As you acknowledge your anger more to yourself and build your sense of self, it will come. Don't pressure yourself.

Dealing with guilt

Even thinking about expressing your feelings can make you feel guilty. After all, those thoughts are in opposition to the many messages about desirable behaviour that you have received all your life.

Many women experience getting what they want, then feeling guilty about it, they feel they have been selfish. Mothers often feel they have no right to time on their own.

Guilt has been called 'the great controller'. It can keep us focusing on the negative (e.g. 'My problem with food continues because I am weak-willed') instead of moving forward to make positive changes. Guilt can be a realistic reaction to how we have behaved or it may arise from unrealistic perceptions of how we should be. For example, we may feel guilty when we know we have behaved badly towards someone. This gives us both useful information – we don't want to behave like that – and the opportunity to do something about it, such as apologizing to the person concerned. But unrealistic, globalized guilt ('I should never have been born', 'I'm no use to anyone', 'I'm weak-willed', 'I'm a bad daughter', and so on) is just crippling and does not create any opportunity for change.

Guilt – binge – guilt – purge – more guilt – low self-esteem and confidence, unrealistic promises to self, I really will stop – binge – guilt . . . This is a cycle familiar to many of us.

EXERCISE 6: IDENTIFYING GUILT

Time: 20 minutes

List the things that you feel guilty about.

Would you expect a friend to feel guilty about these things?

Is it reasonable for one person to expect to be able to do/ cope with all these things?

How easy is it for you to forgive yourself for being less than perfect?

How many Superwomen do you actually know? (You can be sure they have their doubts, fears and guilt, even if they are well-hidden.)

Look at your list again. Cross off everything that you would not expect a friend to feel guilty about.

The guilt that follows a binge can be a real barrier to change. The next exercise aims to help break being stuck in this way.

EXERCISE 7: MAKING DIFFERENT CHOICES

Time: 30 minutes

Think back to the last time you binged, or ate something you felt you shouldn't have. Write a brief description of the situation or recall it in as much detail as you can.

Write the thoughts and feelings you had at the time. Here is an example (Yours might be quite different):

71

Description: *Came home from work. Partner working late. Kids watching TV and squabbling. Mooched around for half an hour. Fed the kids. Got them to bed by eight. Started bingeing. Partner came home while I was vomiting.*
Thoughts and feelings:
Tired when I came home.

Fed up with having to deal with the kids on my own at tea-time.

Lonely – wanted to talk to someone about something that had happened at work.

Irritated with the kids.

Guilty that I didn't have the energy to give them some decent attention.

Relief when kids were in bed – some space.

Lonely, felt fat, ugly, unlovable. I wanted some attention and loving for myself. Never seem to get it from anyone. Kids and partner always want stuff from me.

Feel out of control when I start eating. Can't stop. Stuffing the food in.

Guilt starts – no control over food, rotten mother, can't cope with my life, not a good wife, don't like sex any more, don't even exercise, always tired . . .

When I'm so full my stomach is bursting I feel like I'm on automatic.

Then I'm vomiting.

Hear the front door open – feel guilty, panicky even, at being caught . . .

Look back at your list of thoughts and feelings and identify points at which you could have made a different choice. Could the woman in our example have called a friend when she felt lonely? written down her thoughts and feelings to discuss with her partner or a friend later? planned ways to get the kids involved with meal preparation? brought home prepared food? thought about ways of getting her emotional needs met? considered talking to her partner (it is often worthwhile) or seeking counselling? eaten a meal with the kids? given herself a treat when the kids had gone to bed, like a hot bath? bought herself a food treat on the way home and eaten it when she got in?

Finally, at the point when she was about to binge, could she have gone to Exercise 5 in Chapter 3 (Meeting Unmet

Needs) or Exercise 3 in Chapter 3 (Setting a regular eating pattern)?

The aim of this exercise is to identify all the points at which you made a choice and consider what *other* choices you could make in the future. Having thought about alternatives during an exercise, you will have them in your mind to draw on in the future. If you are keeping a journal you can go back to it at any time to remind yourself of them.

EXERCISE 8: CHANGING EXPECTATIONS

Time: 20 minutes

Guilt is often associated with our having high, unrealistic expectations of ourselves that we cannot possibly meet, so we are set up to fail. Often we have expectations of ourselves that we would never apply to anyone else. We commonly set up diets that we cannot possibly maintain for more than a short period and then blame ourselves for breaking them.

List all the things that you expect of yourself. Here is an example:

Being xx kilos.
Never make mistakes.
Always be good with the kids.
Satisfy my partner sexually.
Work full-time.
Keep the house looking nice.
Always look good.
Be fit.
Dress fashionably.
Be a good cook.
Have lots of friends.

While you do your list, allow plenty of time to think about anything you may have overlooked.

Put a star by the things you do for yourself, and a circle by those for other people. Which of these expectations are causing stress for you? How can you ease off on some of them? Write down some things for yourself that you could replace them with. (For example, 'Have lots of friends' could be scaled down to 'Initiate lunch/coffee/dinner with someone I like but don't know all that well.')

What advice would you give to a friend with your list of expectations?

EXERCISE 9: I'M NOT PERFECT

Time: 30 minutes

Write: *I'm not perfect.* Write the first negative thought that comes into your head (e.g. If I'm not, people will judge me).

Write again: *I'm not perfect*

Write another negative thought.

(This is the same process as that described in Exercise 4, Chapter 3.)

When you run out of negative statements, try writing:
I'm not perfect, and neither is anyone else. And then:
What I am is good enough. (It doesn't matter if you don't really believe it the first time. It is known that repeating these thoughts and ideas can change behaviour and feelings.)

Repeat the process with these statements:
I am not responsible for how other people feel.
I don't have to be slim to be lovable, worthy or successful.
I'm lovable as I am.
I'm worthy just as I am.

Positive statements like the last two can be put up around the house so that you see them every day. If you see them first thing in the morning, they can help you start your day on a positive note.

In *Fat Is A Feminist Issue,* Susie Orbach wrote, 'Food is incapable of making feelings go away. It cannot make things get better, it cannot fill up whatever emptiness there is inside.' The 'emptiness' that Orbach refers to can be relieved by our learning to acknowledge and accept our feelings, and make decisions about how to use the information they give us. If, in doing these exercises, you have identified one feeling that you were not previously aware of, that is really positive. Be aware that recognizing feelings is an opening in itself.

5   Body image and self-esteem

Marcia Germaine has written in *Transforming Body Image
(Learning to love the body you have)*, 'Your body image is
not the same as your physical body. It is the way *you* see and
experience your body, not necessarily how the world sees it –
although how others experience your body can be very
strongly influenced by the verbal and non-verbal messages
you communicate about and through your body. Body
sensations and knowledge of where your body parts are in
relation to each other and in relation to space contribute to
your body image.

'Your body image is experienced on a visual level, how
you see your body; a kinaesthetic level, your felt sense of
being in your body; and an auditory level, how you think
about and talk to yourself about your body. You will
probably find that one or two of these levels need more
rearranging. Perhaps you *feel* comfortable in your body, but
thinking about how you look to others depresses you. Or it
could be the other way around. Maybe you *look* fine to
yourself, but you catch yourself *saying* horrible things to
yourself about your body.

'Your body image encompasses your ideas, feelings,
attitudes and values about your body. Every time you see
yourself in your mirror or catch a fleeting glance reflected in
a store window, every time you look directly at areas of your
body, what you see is coloured by your body image'.

Andrea says: '*My whole life seems to revolve around food
and weight and looks. If I wake up feeling slim and healthy I
go to school feeling great, but if I feel "yuk" I don't want to
go anywhere. I sort of feel like hibernating until I'm slim and
pretty, then I'll go out into the world and everyone will go
"Wow! Andrea's changed!"*

'*I know I shouldn't get paranoid and should enjoy life and
everything. But no matter how much "insight" I have, and no
matter how hard I try, I can't sort myself out and be
contented and happy with me.*'

And Gail: *'I guess you can count me in as bulimic. I'm from a large family and all of us are tall and big (terrible word that, isn't it?). Ever since I can remember they have said I am big. At fourteen I guess I had done most of my growing, so I towered above everyone. With quite a few years of that it got the best of me. I felt unfeminine, always uncomfortable among the dainty wee girls with perfect teeth and beautiful figures and hair. I felt a frump, an elephant. I'd do anything to get out of those social things where I couldn't cope. I always dressed in baggy jeans and at one time I was really overweight and wore men's jeans. I suppose I felt safe and secure'.*

In this chapter we suggest that our bodies are fine, just as they are. (Okay, so you don't believe us. All we ask is that you carry on to the end of the chapter.)

Women have always been admired and judged for how we look, whereas that should be only one part of how we see ourselves and are seen by others. We learn to have an investment in our appearance and to try to look the way others (manufacturers, advertisers, and all those with products to sell) promote as admirable, acceptable, sexually attractive, normal. So naturally we think about it a lot, spend hours and hundreds of dollars "beautifying" ourselves. We worry about what we eat, about getting fat and getting old, both of which will make us "unattractive". The people who matter to us (partners, children, parents, friends) are also getting these messages and so they reinforce them with us. In their caring and concern, they want us to do well, to look right, so that we will be happy and will, possibly, reflect well on them.

There are many things that lead us to feel good about ourselves – deciding that our bodies are okay is one of them. How many of us can truly say we feel really good about ourselves and our bodies? Even those super-slim, super-elegant models that some of us would love to be like, often feel insecure. They worry that their bodies are not good enough and they fear getting fat. How often, when we look at ourselves in the mirror, do we see ourselves as Susie Orbach has said, 'through a tape full of self-denigration'. Most of us share these feelings to some extent, but for those with eating disorders they are often very intense and pervasive.

'I'd be acceptable if I was xx kilos lighter' is a common thinking pattern. Losing the kilos doesn't cure the thought. We can, and often do, think 'If only I could lose another xx kilos.' In a chronic and extreme form, these thought processes are part of anorexic thinking. This ongoing battle with ourselves makes it impossible for us to have a loving relationship with our bodies/ourselves.

Do you ever see images in the media that you recognize as being like yourself?

In the fashion and clothes industry skinny models show off the latest designs, which change every season so we feel compelled to buy in order not to be out-of-date. Their figures don't resemble those of most of us, so even with the best-looking clothes we will never look like them. And we seldom hear about the self-punishment the models endure in order to achieve and maintain their ultra-slim bodies. The popular image of models as sexually fulfilled, happy, well-off, living the high-life (but working hard, of course) often belies the starvation and rigid exercise regimes they have to maintain.

The notion that if our bodies look 'right' we will be happy is continually reinforced. It denies the reality that emotional well-being arises from many sources – health, job satisfaction, positive relationships, enough money, supportive friends, a sense of self-worth. The message we get is that if we can get our bodies 'right' all of these will fall into place, which is just not true. If it were, all the thin people in the world would be happy! In Western Society at present, almost no one is allowed to feel satisfied with their body the way it is. Given the social/cultural milieu we live in, it is not surprising so many of us hate our bodies. To compound matters, as women we learn that it is egotistical and boastful to say anything good about ourselves or our bodies. The emphasis is on how we can improve our appearance, rather than on appreciating ourselves as we are.

EXERCISE 1: DO I LIKE MY BODY?

Time: 5 minutes
Where would you place yourself on this line, or continuum?

0 _____ 10
I don't accept   I do accept
my body as it is   my body as it is

   Have you put yourself further along the line than you
would have before you started this book? Can you imagine
putting yourself right up at the 10 end?

EXERCISE 2: I DON'T HAVE TO BE SLIM TO ENJOY LIFE

Time: 30 minutes
Think about the things in your life that you think would be
different if you were slim. Write them down. (Don't include
the things that are outside your control, like finding clothes
that fit. In this exercise we focus on things you *can* do.)

   Think about giving yourself permission to include these
things in your life right now. For example, if you wrote 'I
would be socializing more' or 'I would be in a relationship
now if I were thinner,' imagine working towards these, now.
Start by sitting or lying down in a relaxed posture. Play
some soothing music if you wish. (Hard rock isn't soothing!)
Take several deep breaths and become aware as your body
relaxes. Now try creating a scene in your mind where you
experience yourself, just as you are, with your body the same
as it is now, but doing some of the things you have listed.
Imagine, too, that in your fantasy a whole range of body
sizes and shapes were appreciated just for how they were, so
there was no external pressure on you about slimness. Give
yourself the pleasure of engaging in your fantasies in your
mind. Use all your sensations – seeing, hearing, touching,
smelling, tasting, feeling – to make the imagining as rich as
possible.

   When you feel ready to leave this visualization, become
aware of your body and the things around you. These are
images you can dip into at any time to help you tackle things
you may be avoiding or putting off. You can also begin
taking steps to make some of them happen.

Write down three things you could do in the next month to work towards them. Remind yourself that there is no reason why you should restrict your life, and the possibilities that are open to you, simply because of your current attitudes towards your body image.

EXERCISE 3: NEGATIVE MESSAGES

Time: 30 minutes

Think about the negative messages you have in your head, along the lines of 'I'll only be lovable if I'm fifty-five kilos, or less', 'I can only like myself if I have thirteen percent or less body fat.'

Write them in a column on one side of a paper or a page in your journal. Spend a full ten minutes on this so that you are sure you bring up all the negatives.

Turn each negative statement into a positive one and write it in the other column. For example:

I'll only be lovable if I'm xx kilos or less.	I'm lovable just as I am
I can only like myself if I have xx% or less body fat.	There are lots of likeable things about me – my laugh, my intelligence, my generosity . . .

It might be hard to actually believe the positive statements at first, but the more you repeat the exercise, the more you will come to believe them!

Nobody's Perfect

But Parts of me are excellent

EXERCISE 4: MY BODY IS OKAY

Time: 15 minutes
Write: *'My body is okay the way it looks now'*.
Now write a negative reaction you have to that statement,
e.g. 'Rubbish! my thighs are too fat.'
Repeat: *My body is okay the way it looks now*
Write another negative response: e.g. I hate my double chin.

When you can't think of any more negative reactions re-write each as a positive statement, e.g. 'I have lovely, strong/plump/shapely thighs.'

Finish by writing *'My body is unique and mine and it's okay'* several times, even if you can't completely believe it.

How are you getting on with all this positive thinking? It can be hard when you are so used to thinking that your body is awful, and may bring up some feelings of anxiety. But you have to start somewhere to change your thought patterns into more accepting and positive ones and the anxiety will pass. Remember: *No Body Is Perfect*.

EXERCISE 5: LOOKING GOOD

Time: 5 minutes, as often as you like
Stand in front of a mirror, look at yourself and make three positive statements to yourself about the way you look. For example, 'My thighs are part of me. They are strong and serve an essential function for my body.' Develop as many statements as you can about how these parts of your body work for you.

Initially, it will be difficult to get past thoughts like 'Yuk, fat, ugly thighs' or 'Fat ugly stomach,' or 'I hate my flabby arms.' Concentrate on the functions of these parts of your body, how they work for you, e.g. 'My stomach is part of me. It processes the food that keeps me alive and gives me information about how I am feeling, about what my emotions are.'

Remember, we have options about how we think about our bodies: a half empty milk bottle can also be described as half full!

EXERCISE 6: LOOKING BACK

Time: 15 minutes, more if you decide to write your responses.
We are all likely to have childhood messages that are
entrenched in our conditioning. Often we act as though these
are true.

Can you reflect back on these messages or 'scripts' and
identify them? Were you told you were 'too tall', 'chubby',
'too shy', 'too talkative', 'not feminine enough – a tomboy',
'the bad/ugly one in the family'? Acknowledge these and see
if you can begin to put them aside, realizing that as an adult
person you can have a lot more control over your life. If this
seems really hard, try to identify what is blocking the way –
for example, some unmet needs as a child. One woman felt
that she have never been 'mothered', so through counselling
she had to learn to 'mother' herself ('I can do for myself what
my mother never did for me').

If your childhood includes any sort of abuse (sexual,
physical or emotional) or trauma that feels very painful, an
exercise like this may not be adequate to help you deal with
it fully. If it brings up painful issues, consider getting more
help.

EXERCISE 7: TELEVISION IMAGES

Time: A few minutes here and there
The images of women that we are presented with cover a
very narrow range, as discussed earlier. This exercise is to
alert you to how this occurs in practice and suggest some
action you can take.

While watching TV, note the way the women are
portrayed. Do they make decisions and act on them? What is
important – what they do, or how they present themselves?
What things are they doing? What are their concerns? Are
they trivial or important? Do you see any women like
yourself? What roles do you see women in? How often do
you see women in the roles of sex object? demented
housewife? perfect cook?

Do you feel guilty or inadequate because you do not have
the 'right' figure, as shown in the advertisements? Try telling
yourself, 'These images of women are contrived and artificial.

It is not necessary for me to be like that. (Or I wouldn't want to be like that).'

Advertisers are *very* sensitive to public opinion. Write to them about any ads that you find offensive. They may not admit it, but they do take notice, especially if they get several letters – so organize your friends.

Perfectionist Expectations

Anorexic and bulimic women place very high expectations on themselves and their bodies. These tend to be of a perfectionist nature: 'I'm not good enough unless I'm two stone lighter', 'I shouldn't ever break my diet', 'I should always be sociable, extroverted and outgoing, even when I don't feel like it,' etc. The response pattern is all or nothing. If the woman binges, the thinking tends to be 'I've broken my diet. I have had one biscuit so I might as well have the whole packet. My whole day is down the tubes. I am a failure.' This thinking is a sure recipe for an ongoing battle with oneself and definitely sets the stage for failure.

EXERCISE 8: CHALLENGING PERFECTIONIST THOUGHTS

Time: 15 minutes

Write a list of the ways in which you expect yourself to be perfect. For example:

I should always be good-tempered.

I mustn't ever eat chocolate.

Change each one into a more moderate statement. For example:

I am allowed to be crabby.

I can eat chocolate when I feel like it.

Get into the habit of doing this every day, in those odd moments – sitting on the bus, waiting for someone. Identify an absolute expectation you have of yourself (e.g. I mustn't make mistakes) and re-phrase it into a more moderate expectation (e.g. Everyone makes mistakes, including me.)

Self-esteem

In our society, body image is heavily emphasized as a source of self-esteem. To deal with self-esteem, we need to go beyond our feelings about our bodies and discover our feelings about our whole selves. We are more than our bodies.

Iris Barrow writes in *Know Your Strength and Be Confident*, 'It is necessary for us to have a healthy self-esteem in order to function well. The lack of it can limit us and even prevent us from reaching our potential as loving, caring, feeling human beings. Our self-concept – the way we see and feel about ourselves – depends very much on the degree of love we have for ourselves. The more we have, the better 'balanced out' emotionally we will be and the better we will be able to relate to and accept other people.

'There are many facets to self-love. It embraces our self-respect and self-esteem; the way we value ourselves as people, our feelings of self-worth, the way in which we care for and about ourselves, and the degree to which we like, and above all, accept ourselves. It also includes our tolerance towards others, an inner security, and even in many instances, the degree to which we are self-motivated. These things however, are just the starting-point. The degree of love we bear ourselves affects every aspect of our lives, from our self-concept to the way we relate to other people. It has a marked bearing on our inner confidence. Healthy self-love is the basis upon which all else is built. It is the foundation stone for our confidence, integrity, relationships, compassion and caring – and even at times our ability to succeed and achieve.'

Western society places a lot of value on what we can *do* rather than who we *are*. Yet a sense of being and a sense of achieving need to combine to produce self-esteem. How one thinks leads to feelings and feelings lead to actions. Here are some common patterns which lead to negative feelings and a poor view of oneself.

1. *Rigid thinking:* 'I binge, therefore I'm a bad person', 'I'm not slim (enough) therefore I'm unattractive', or 'I forgot again . . . I'm a dummy'. In these statements, the woman is using one piece of behaviour to label herself. Labelling is a common result of this kind of thinking, it's like wearing a T-shirt message, 'I'm a failure, not worth much.'

2. *Grey-tinted glasses:* Some people view the world in a pessimistic way. For example, 'I'm overweight . . . no one

will be interested in me', or 'I'm weak-willed . . . I haven't succeeded with any of the diets I've tried'.

3. *Kangaroo jumping:* This means jumping to conclusions. 'He didn't ring, therefore he doesn't care about me', or 'If she knew about my problem, she'd think I was a total freak'. Obviously, there are several possible explanations for these situations, but a woman with low self-esteem is likely to choose one that is negative about herself.

4. *Telescopic vision:*
   (a) *Viewing mistakes:* This person will use the telescope the normal way and so blow the situation out of all proportion. 'I haven't got a relationship . . . I'm unlovable', or 'I can't remember names . . . I'm stupid'.
   (b) *Viewing strengths:* This person will turn the telescope around the other way, making herself appear much smaller. 'I've completed my training course . . . but that's nothing, anyone could have done it', or 'I've really taken care of myself today . . . but it's no big deal, really'.

5. *The slave driver:* Many people become their own slave drivers. 'I should have done better', or 'I ought to be perfect', or 'I must please everyone', or 'I must weigh xxx kilos'. These are some of the messages we pick up as we grow up and internalize into self-criticism. At times some of these messages are appropriate, but they often over-ride our thinking, and control our lives. A person who doesn't live up to these commands all the time feels guilty and a failure. Her sense of self-worth drops.

6. *Cyclical thinking:* Thoughts of low self-esteem can go round and round in our heads in a vicious cycle, as this diagram of the Low Self-Esteem Cycle shows:

You think poorly of yourself, concentrating on your weaknesses and ignoring your strengths.

The way they treat you confirms your own view of yourself.

You send out the messages to others that you're inferior.

Others believe you and treat you accordingly.

my mask helps me to get to know myself better and get closer to the other person.

Accept myself. There are things I don't particularly like about myself, things I wish were different. Those things I cannot change I will accept and even value as parts of myself.

Love myself. This will make me more able to love others - for many of us this is one of the hardest things to do. We need to be on the alert for those negative thoughts and feelings that creep back into our minds, and to turn then into affirmations. Spending five minutes every morning saying positive and loving things to ourselves can be a good starter, as in The Good Self-Esteem Cycle:

I think positively of myself,
affirming my strengths but
aware of my weaknesses

They way they treat me confirms
my own view of myself

I send out messages
to others that I'm OK

Others believe me and
treat me accordingly

To sustain a good self-image, we need acceptance, affirmation, positive feedback, love, respect, hugs etc, from those close to us. No one has a cast-iron self-esteem all the time and we are particularly vulnerable at times of change like adolescence, menopause, relationship break-up, when losing a job. For those of us who are 'different' through being from a minority racial group, lesbian, fat, or with a disability (or any combination of these and other 'differences'), the generally negative attitudes of society can be an extra burden that we have to deal with to develop our self-esteem. For some women, it is empowering to begin to fight some of these attitudes.

In this chapter we have asked you to explore some really deep-seated feelings and attitudes. Many of the body-image exercises can be done over and over with increasing benefit. You decide which ones are most valuable for you and repeat them as often as they are giving you something new.

Self-esteem is crucial to our whole sense of well-being, so give this section a lot of attention. Use your journal, or note-taking, to explore how the ideas we have presented apply to you. You are likely to gain more and more benefit from returning to this section.

6 Relationships

Elizabeth's story

'I started making myself sick about six years ago and have been doing so regularly ever since.

'I'm in a steady relationship and have two children, one five years old and the other eleven months. I'm thirty-two years old. Every day I feel as though I'm damaging my health. I often feel very dizzy and have constant headaches. I don't really have anyone I can talk to about my eating problems and would hate anyone to find out.

'I'm always being admired for being reasonably slim, only no one realizes what I go through to stay this way. When I was younger, I was overweight. Someone said how good I would look if only I was slimmer. I never really managed to stay on a calorie-controlled diet.

'Before I became pregnant, I had been vomiting for about a year or more. When I realized I was having a child, I stopped. Needless to say, since I no longer vomited or fasted, I gained a lot of weight during pregnancy, most of which remained after the birth. For two years following my child's birth I lived with his father in a strange, cold sort of relationship. He just didn't see me as a "woman", which sounds ridiculous, but we stopped having sex, stopped talking. I got a night job and took care of my son during the day.

'One day I suddenly decided to lose weight and started alternative vomiting and fasting. I lost weight and met someone else.

'My son's father moved out and I continued seeing my new man. He admired my body and forever commented on how "nice" and slim I was. I have since had his child and we all live in a very loving happy environment, although staying slim and attractive to him is more difficult than he could ever believe or imagine. I love him dearly and hate to think that in such a feministic society – much of which I feel very strongly about – I'm being so ridiculous about my body. I

*feel foolish, guilty, the oppressed female, etc . . . Yet I can't
stop this overwhelming desire to stay slim, regardless of how
many children I give birth to, or how old I am.*

*'Everything and everyone is so competitive. I put on
weight so easily – I couldn't cope with being fat. I feel I'd
lose everything I love. Logically I know that's ridiculous, but
I've been overweight and life was awful. Since being
reasonably slim, my life has changed so much. People are
different towards me. I'm terrified things will change if I gain
weight. I think I'd lose my self-respect. I can't bear myself
like that. I even made myself vomit when I was pregnant
with my second child, which filled me with guilt. The
thought of putting self-image in priority to my baby's health
– God, I can't believe it. I can't ever see an end to all this.*

*'I'm often very depressed about what I'm doing to myself,
but it just seems to be my life – secretly.*

*'My man goes to a gym and is very body conscious – he
hates fat. But he himself consumes enormous amounts of
food. I've often tried to talk to him, but he always says he
would never get fat and if he did he would just magically lose
it. He is the first man I have ever truly loved and I get
frightened at the thought of gaining weight, for fear he
would change towards me. I like the way he admires me.*

*'He says it wouldn't make any difference to him if I gained
a little weight, only he likes me just as I am. "Just as I am" is
very hungry and I wish it would all stop. It's controlling me.'*

We may not immediately connect our relationships with the
people around us to an eating disorder, but they are part of
our social/cultural environment and of our emotional lives –
two of the three strands we have talked about. Just as our
problem with food can serve some purpose for us, it can also
be a deflection from other issues for those around us.

There is nothing to be gained from trying to blame either
ourselves or someone else for our problem with food. Just as
we affect the people around us, their behaviour, values and
attitudes influence and affect us.

EXERCISE 1: THE PEOPLE CLOSE TO ME[10]

Time: 30 minutes.

The purpose of this exercise is to give you information about your relationships and clarify the ways that other people may be involved in your relationship with food. It may help you identify problem areas for you in your relationships. The rest of this chapter will give you more ideas about how to do this.

In your journal list each significant person in your life now and any from the past you have unresolved feelings about. Now write your responses to the following statements, going through the sequence for each person in turn. (The questions are adapted from a family therapy book, so they are focused on family relationships. However, they can be usefully applied to any close relationship.) Some of your responses may be in the past tense.

1. My relationship with XXX does/does not involve shifts between almost-suffocating closeness and almost total abandonment.

2. XXX is over-protective and hinders me from making my own decisions.

3. People in my family always react the same way. I know what they are going to say and think of me.

4. The conflicts I had/have with XXX have never really been resolved.

5. I feel very involved in my parents' relationship with each other, I think about it a lot and discuss it with each or both of them.

6. The only people I can rely on at all for emotional support are members of my immediate family (parents, brothers, sisters).

7. I feel as though I let my family down if I don't look right and don't always do the right thing in public.

8. We use food and eating experiences as a way of communicating: mealtimes are times when people's feelings show in their behaviour and can be very tense and negative if someone is upset or angry. I often feel tense around food.

Conflict

Conflict is an unavoidable part of any close relationship. Conflicts arise out of differences which are accentuated when we are living with or relating to people closely. Conflicts are most often resolved successfully when there is goodwill and commitment to the relationship between the people concerned.

One model for dealing with conflict presents three options:
1. *Capitulation.* One person gives in to the other completely. This is satisfactory if it is a free choice to go the other's way and if the other person takes turns in "giving in".

2. *Compromise.* Neither party gives in completely but both create options and end up with a solution that satisfies them.

3. *Co-existence.* There is agreement to accept the difference after sincerely trying to resolve it. This can be a hard one, but can help us to appreciate and understand each other more deeply.

EXERCISE 2: CONFLICT

Time: 10 minutes.
Think about yourself for a few minutes.

Do you tend to avoid conflict or do you try to face it until it is resolved?

How do you usually settle disagreements – by capitulation, compromise or co-existence?

Are you satisfied with your pattern or would you like to vary it sometimes?

Think about the last time you had a conflict. (Write brief details if you wish.) Are you satisifed with the outcome? Do you think it would have made any difference if you had tried a different option from the list above?

During the process of understanding more about your relationship with food, you may become aware that you use food to stuff down feelings when you are faced with a conflict. You may take out your frustrations by eating when someone makes a comment about your body or weight. It is important to see these comments for what they are – someone else's opinion, reflecting *their* values, rather than being a failing in you.

Some mothers can be over-concerned about how their daughters look – they have learnt that it is a reflection on them and, as well, they usually want the 'best' for us. We can educate the people around us by refusing to accept these comments, by responding 'That really upsets me and makes me feel like I'm nothing if I don't look right' or 'I want you to accept me the way I am' or 'Why is the size I am so important to you?'

Parents, partners and friends may need to examine their own attitudes. Why should it matter to them if you are a few pounds heavier than they think is ideal? Where did they get these opinions and ideas from? Consider asking them to read Chapter 9: For Friends and Relations.

EXERCISE 3: WHO'S INVOLVED?

Time: 20 minutes to set up, and then a few minutes a day for as long as you do it.

This exercise is a variation on logging binge-eating/bulimic episodes. It takes your relationships into account. If you are still logging from Chapter 2, change to this form. If you are not and you are still bingeing, start up again using these headings:

O the place where the binge occurred
O those who were involved, before and after the episode
O their responses
O the way in which others were helpful or not
O your feelings before and after the episode
O all the foods that you ate
O the technique of purging (if you did)

It is useful to acknowledge to yourself any conflict with family, at work, with friends, even if you don't feel you can change the situation right away. Recognizing that it is a conflict, and accepting your own feelings about it, is affirming in itself and a step towards change.

Dealing with conflict

When we are in a conflict we can fight fair or fight dirty.

Ways of fighting dirty	How to fight clean
1. Attack the person	1. Attack the issue.
2. Bring up old issues.	2. Stay with the issues. Hold no grudges.
3. Introduce diversions, 'red herrings'.	3. Deal with the topic in hand.
4. Don't hear the other person out.	4. Really listen: check out what is being said.
5. Use physical force or the threat of it.	5. Don't give any signals that you might use force.
6. Shout, bully, threaten.	6. Express your feelings.
7. Have a 'temper tantrum', sulk, let emotions control the situation.	7. Deal with your anger first. Focus on the issue.
8. Put the other person down, criticize: 'You're always . . .', 'You never . . .'	8. Build the other person up. 'Were you saying . . .'
9. Manipulate by saying/ doing things you know will trigger certain emotions.	9. Keep communication straight and direct.
10. Attack the other's weak spots.	10. Avoid the other's tender areas.
11. Fight in public.	11. Do it in private.
12. Use 'you' statements, blaming, accusing.	12. Use 'I' statements.

What other ways can you think of?

If the other person fights dirty, consider having a third party present, such as a counsellor.

EXERCISE 4: IT'S NOT MY PROBLEM

Time: 15 minutes.

Look at the chart you did for Exercise 3. Identify remarks that have been made to you by other people and how they left you feeling. Record your feelings like this (we have put some sample answers in italics. Yours may be quite different):

Situation: *Family dinner.*
Remark from: *Brother – 'You're piling it on a bit, Fran.'*
Feelings: *Fat, awful, embarrassed.*
What you did to cope: *Pushed food around plate, didn't eat any. Didn't look at anyone for ages.*
What could you have done instead? *Could have ignored him and talked to someone else. Told him off. Said, 'I enjoy my food, isn't that great?'*

When someone makes a disparaging remark about your body, practise thinking, 'That's his/her problem' (even if you don't believe it yourself at first).

EXERCISE 5: AFFIRMING MYSELF

Time: 10 minutes.

Write: *I accept myself as I am.*
Write your negative response: *One little comment from someone and I feel awful.*
Write the original statement again.
Write another thought.
Follow this pattern until you don't have any new negative thoughts, then write the original statement several times.

Sharing our problems about food – enlisting support

Many of the women who took part in Jasbindar's survey expressed shame about the behaviour with food that had led them to behave secretly about it. In many cases, completing the questionnaire was the first time they had revealed the problem to anyone and they were anxious that no one close to them should find out.

These fears are common. As well, we might fear that

others will feel as badly towards us as we feel about ourselves, and that if we tell the people around us, we will have even less control. They will tell us what to eat and what not to eat, our behaviour will be monitored.

Another obstacle for some of us is the feeling that we are the 'strong one', the one to whom other people come for help and support. It can be difficult to get out of this role, to talk about our own needs and frustrations, and ask for help and support for ourselves. Often it is worth making the effort to break down this barrier, as it can lead to closer and more real relationships.

If we are going to tell people about our problems with food, we also need to be able to tell them what we want from them. For example, don't say 'Don't pay a lot of attention to what I eat, that just makes me feel worse', but try saying 'I would appreciate it if you would reinforce the things I say I am pleased about, and help me sometimes when I want to distract myself from thinking about food.'

Tell only those people you already have a relationship of trust with. Just because you've told your partner/sister/ friend/flatmate doesn't mean that you have to follow their advice or that they know better than you what you need. If they can support you in making your own decisions, that's great.

Try to be really specific in telling the people around you what you want from them. Try to believe that you are entitled to ask for what you need, that you don't have to accept what is offered, just because it is offered. If the help and support you need is being offered, take it; don't turn it away!

If a return to the family home invariably triggers binge behaviour, can you talk with your parents about this? Be aware that it may be threatening to them – if they cannot change, or if you don't think it's worth stirring things up, what can you do for yourself to change the pattern? Take a friend with you? Be very clear before you go what the triggers are (e.g. your mother still treats you as a child, your father is disapproving of your lesbian lifestyle, you feel sad about the emotionally empty relationship you have with your parents, or about the relationship they have with each other)? Accept the limitations, accept that you will have bad feelings and that is quite natural. Where there are things that you cannot change, it is often best to acknowledge them and, although this is not easy, concentrate on getting on with your own life in the best way that you can. Maybe you could limit the time of your visit, and plan to do something soon after that is positive for you, like visiting a supportive friend or spending more time on your own doing something you find rewarding.

Are there any positive statements that you could start practising now for the next time you visit your family (e.g. 'I am a person in my own right', 'I am a strong person in charge of my life', 'My parents have their own opinions and attitudes and I don't have to buy into them')? Find some that suit you.

Amy's story

'I started bingeing when I was at high school and living with my mother. We frequently went on fad diets, usually to no avail. I have always, even when very little, been plump and gone up and down in weight, and was conscious of it.

'I have since married and only started gaining weight again in the last year or so. For the last year I have been dieting, bingeing and vomiting. The last few months have been the worst. If I get angry or upset, I eat, then vomit and cry and say I'll never do it again. If I eat one bad thing I am away. I don't know what happens, I don't even think about what I'm doing.

'A couple of weeks ago I was very down and tearful. My husband finally got out of me what I had been doing. He was very good, understanding and sympathetic. Although I do feel ashamed, especially as he feels I have lied to him and also spent our money on food that has been wasted.

'He told me to see my doctor, which I did, but I wasn't really sure she cared. I got the impression she thought I was pathetic and she made me feel stupid and childish. She said I should join yoga to relax, and that was that. She asked me what I was going to do about it.

'I really don't know why I do it as I like healthy food and want to be slim. I'm twenty-four years old.

'I feel better when I don't eat at all, but as soon as I do, I'm away, and eat as though it's the last meal I will ever have. My husband works late shifts and I finish work at

3 pm. I thought this was the reason I sat and ate, but I still do it. It's not as though I even enjoy the food or want it, I just have to eat it and then vomit, thinking I will be good tomorrow.

'I am a waitress and if I pick just once I find I am thinking, well I won't lose weight today anyway, I might was well eat what I want. Then I panic and vomit again. I have got to the stage where I am putting weight on anyway, which makes me depressed, and the vicious cycle continues.

'I have very little self-respect left. I don't like my own company and I cry a lot. My husband feels helpless, because if I can't help myself, what can he do? I may never get his trust back. I'm happy when I'm in control and lose weight but as soon as I gain weight I feel miserable and have to vomit to punish myself for eating. If we have biscuits in the house, which is rare, I have to eat them all to get rid of them so they are no longer a threat. This makes my husband very angry. He used to count them before he knew what I was doing. I just wish I could stop and feel that it must be psychological, as when I do it, I switch off. My marriage is suffering and I tend to find security in what I'm doing, which is wrong.'

Professional help

If the conflicts and problems of eating just seem too great for you to handle on your own, don't feel embarrassed or fearful about seeking professional help. A professional – psychologist, therapist or psychotherapist – will not provide a magical cure but they can help you to explore your problem and provide new insights. They can make helpful practical suggestions, and be affirming and supportive.

Be choosy about who you go to – not all doctors or therapists have a good understanding of eating disorders, as Amy discovered. Check out your local women's centre or women's health centre, or ask around the women you know. Also, see the resource list at the end of this book.

Don't feel that you have to stick with the first person you go to. Trust your own intuitions about whether they have anything to offer you. Don't go back if you are prescribed diet pills, if it is suggested that you will grow out of this, if you feel diminished in any way by the person's attitude, or if they don't listen to what you have to say. Look for someone else.

Make specific requests about what you want from a therapist. Ask them to explain what their approach is. Again, trust your intuitions, both as to how you react to them and what they tell you. Have goals for yourself – discuss these and evaluate whether the therapist is helping you to achieve them. It's not a matter of putting yourself in their hands, but of seeing what they have that can be helpful to you.

Cost may be a factor. Check if the professional you are seeing has a sliding scale of fees, related to client income. Hospital and community mental health services may be free, but they are very thinly spread. You could check out your area for community mental health centres, women counsellors (particularly those with a feminist perspective), or existing support groups. Community houses and Citizens Advice Bureaux may also have information.

The process of change is in your hands. Be kind to yourself. Any gains, like bingeing less, or bingeing without purging, are *real* successes and stepping-stones towards further change.

7   Creating a New Pathway

creating a new pathway

So far we have focused on dealing with issues surrounding food, which has involved exploring our roles, emotions, and health. In this chapter we widen the focus. While food can be an important and pleasurable aspect of living, it is by no means our entire life. 'No woman can live by "bread" alone!' Here we take a brief look at stress management and spirituality, and hope that we provide some positive lines for you to explore aspects of your own life.

One day at a time

Even after you start dealing with your eating problem, you are likely to have setbacks or days when you binge. You may see this as a failure, dooming you to a bleak future. In the early days of change it is important to focus on just the day ahead. If it goes badly, see it as just that, a bad day, rather than total failure. There is also a choice within the day – if you binge in the morning, you can still have a good afternoon and evening. Or if you had a good eating day and binged in the evening, remind yourself that the evening was the only disappointing part of the day. Old habits die hard, so keep giving yourself credit and rewards for every little success.

The first exercise in this chapter is a beginning in taking the focus off food. What can you do instead of making a crisis out of a setback? As you free yourself from domination by food, you will have choices to make about what you will do with the time, energy and money that was being taken up. Your life can become one where you enjoy food, enjoy socializing with or without it, where food is part of your life but not dominating it.

And if you binge occasionally, so what?

EXERCISE 1: CREATING CHOICES

Time: 10 minutes
What is your strongest thought/feeling after a binge? Write it down.

If it involves hopelessness, despair or failure ('I've done it again, the day is wasted', 'I'll never get rid of this') try to rewrite it as something like 'That was a bad session, but it's over now, and I can get on with something else'.

The purpose of this exercise is to stop yourself from turning single actions into total disasters. Practise becoming aware of your mind doing this, and saying *Stop!*, acknowledging what has happened, and moving on. For example: 'I ate all that cake. I feel so fat and awful.' *Stop* 'I ate that cake and it was really nice. Now I'll go and talk to Joan.'

Remember, at every point you have a choice to look at your actions around food differently. If you start to binge and stop, or if you don't purge, or if you eat less in a binge than you used to, congratulate yourself, give yourself a reward. You don't have to be perfect in changing your eating habits, everyone slips up – you can even decide to 'give in' to a desire to binge. If you have a good day, or several in a row, pat yourself on the back. List things that you would see as rewards and make a point of giving them to yourself – have a bath, listen to music, take a walk, watch TV, visit a friend, buy yourself something if you can, go to bed with a book – you can keep adding to your list. Try keeping a 'nurturing box' in which you can put ideas for rewards written on pieces of paper as a resource for those times when you just can't think of anything to reward yourself with.

Some women find developing positive rituals (often involving elements like candles, water, flowers, or shells) for themselves helpful. Books like *Mother Wit* by Diane Mariechild (Crossing Press, New York) and *Dreaming the Dark* by Starhawk (Beacon Press, Boston) have many examples. Some find the beauties of nature, large or small, soothing and healing.

What do I want out of life?

As women we have not been encouraged to have any sort of active life plan. A consistent theme in some women's responses to Jasbindar's survey was their lack of a sense of direction and meaning in their lives. The prevalent thinking was passive, like a hope that 'something exciting will happen one day'. This thinking is similar to the attitude that life will really begin and become enjoyable when we are slim. While we are waiting, whether it be for prince(ss) charming, to be slim, or for something neat to happen, we are not living fully. And we may be missing the opportunities around us.

Think about what you would like life to be like – this morning, today, this week, in a month, a year. Are you able to do anything towards achieving any of these goals right now? Think about it as a decision you are making about your life. If you are going to go on waiting, *decide* that that is what you will do.

EXERCISE 2: TODAY IS THE BEGINNING OF THE REST OF MY LIFE

Time: 30 minutes

Write a list of ten things you would like to have done before the end of your life. Put these in a column on one side of a page. Alongside each, write what you have already done to achieve each one, and what you plan to do. It doesn't matter if you haven't done anything towards achieving the things on your list as the purpose of the exercise is to spend some time thinking about your life as a whole. And it's nice to have a few fantasies, too! Though some women find it hard to want anything – they have learnt that if you don't want anything you don't get disappointed.

Again, make decisions whether or not to act on each item on your list right now. Action involves taking risks. The only way to not take any risks is to do nothing! You decide.

Spirituality

Donna: *'It took me a great deal of courage to acknowledge that some important things were missing in my life and that my focus on food was a substitute and a distraction'.*
Tina: *'I know that I have to merge a balance between my body, emotion, intellect and spirituality for me to feel good about myself'.*

Spiritually is an important dimension of our being human. It is something we all have, even though we may not be tuned in to it. Spirituality is about having a world view and a sense of there being something greater than us as individuals, that makes sense and gives meaning to life. It gives us a deeper sense of awareness, a perspective on and connectedness to things and people around us, and helps us grow. We each have a unique sense of spirituality. Prayer, meditation, seeking solace in nature, reflective silence, rituals, membership of a spiritual group or community are all different means of expressing this dimension of our selves.

Do you know what your spiritual basis is? Reflect on this for a while.

In terms of our three-stranded approach to eating disorders, we believe that spirituality is most closely tied in with our emotions. For example, it is often through our feelings that we can become aware of and experience our sense of spirituality. However, spirituality permeates the other two strands as well. As one woman has said, 'Who I am is part of my spirituality – my body is part of this spirituality too'.

Our spirituality and our degree of wellness are closely linked. Wellness requires healthy development in all areas of life: becoming a whole person. Wholeness doesn't mean we have arrived, but that we are growing and maturing, with no department of our personality neglected. While some aspect of our life may be particularly developed, this must not be at the expense of the rest.

100

One of the key concepts in wellness is balance: neither excessive development in one aspect of life, nor too little in another area. Important examples of this principle are maintaining a balance between right brain and left brain functions, and balance between the stress response and the relaxation response in order to maintain optimum health.

When we apply this principle to our lives as women, it can illustrate how seldom we consider our own needs. Balance in your life may seem like a wild dream at present, with much you cannot control (e.g. you can't get a job you want, or you have pre-school children and no access to childcare), but acknowledging that you have needs and identifying them is a beginning for change.

Another way to use this principle is to identify de-stressing ways of thinking and behaving:

De-Stressors

PSYCHOLOGICAL	INTELLECTUAL	PHYSICAL
O self-acceptance	O positive thinking	O learn to listen to your body
O self-awareness	O clarification of priorities	O healthy eating
O self-nurturing	O planning	O adequate exercise
O personal growth	O realistic goal setting	O sport
O self-change	O delegation of work	O physical touch/ sex
O building self-esteem	O learning to say 'no'	O muscle relaxation
O warmth	O assertion training	O relaxation breathing
O seeking counselling		

Stress Skills

SOCIAL	EMOTIONAL	SPIRITUAL
O sharing with a friend (crying, laughing)	O releasing emotions	O singing
	O developing intimacy	O dancing
O support groups		O prayer
O socializing	O learning to 'switch off'	O meditation
O entertaining		O praise
O helping others	O solitude/space	O rituals
O community involvement	O taking time out	
	O creative hobbies	
O balanced life	O music	

If you have persisted in reading this book up to this point, you are making great progress! Think about the parts of the book and the ideas that you have found helpful. Write a list of them, with your own thoughts on how you can use and develop them further to help yourself.

Remember, any change in behaviour is difficult to achieve, so it's really important that you give yourself lots of credit and praise for all your successes, even the ones that seem quite small.

Creating a new pathway is a challenge. It can mean re-establishing ordinary eating habits, dealing with emotions as they occur, learning to value yourself and maintaining a sense of control in what often seems a crazy, oppressive and unsupportive world. But the rewards are great and not the least of these is that food *can* become a pleasant and enjoyable part of your life.

Our best wishes go with you. Remember, nobody's perfect, but we all have excellent bits.

8 Self-Help Groups

Women who are just coming out of bulimic behaviour often have an urge to help other women who are going through the same thing. They can offer very valuable help. Self-help groups, where people with similar experiences get together, are one of the most useful means of help and support.

Setting up a support group

In setting up a support group, there are certain things that you need to think about:

O Will it be a woman-only group? We think this is necessary. Exploring issues around role models and sexism and sharing personal experiences openly is impossible in a mixed group. Partners, friends, parents and other family members can be encouraged to form a group for themselves.

O Will the group be open (anyone can join at any time) or closed (no new members accepted)? Our experience is that it is better to close a group so that trust can develop and the group does not have to keep going back to the beginning for new members. If the group is using this book, for example, it can progress through the various themes and chapters.

O How many should there be in a group? Six is a really good number, less than four requires an absolute commitment from all members and more than eight is too big. It can be good to start with eight, if that is possible, as one or two will usually drop out.

O How often? Once a week is probably best, but fortnightly can work too. Using homework exercises in between is a good way to keep up interest and involvement.

O Facilitation – one or two, or everyone taking a turn? Because many bulimic women lack self-esteem, confidence and a sense of structure, it often works best to have one or two people with facilitation skills take this responsibility. As time goes on, others may feel like practising these skills.

○ How long should each meeting be? About two hours seems to work best.

○ Use a professional, or not? That's for the group to decide. If there is a woman available, it may be good to use her skills for the first few sessions, as long as she does not become the focus of the group and the 'expert'. The professional could have a co-facilitator who is an on-going member of the group. A recovered bulimic, who can be a role model for other members, is often a good choice. In a self-help group, it is important that each member feel that she can play both roles – supporter and supported, helper and helped.

○ One group for all eating disorders? Our experience is that bulimic and anorexic women benefit from separate groups. While there are things in common, the group dynamic seems to work more successfully if they are separate.

○ How do we structure sessions? It is often best to have a theme. Or a group could work its way through this book, using each chapter as a focus for one or two weeks.

○ For how long should we keep meeting as a group? An initial eight-week commitment is enough for most people. At the end of this time, group members can decide if they want to go on meeting. Some 'buddy pairs' may have formed, or a small group of three or four may want to go on meeting for longer if the whole group decides to finish. The group may decide to have a follow-up meeting in three months and another in six months.

○ Where do we meet? At a community house, women's centre, or someone's house (rotating is possible)?. The venue needs space, seating and privacy. Not everyone can provide these in their home, so care should be taken in setting a rotating location that no woman feels that she cannot remain in the group because she has no suitable meeting space, or her home situation makes it impossible.

○ Where do the group members come from? One or two women have to be willing to act as contact people and then the possibility of the group can be advertised anywhere women are likely to see a notice, through local networks, community houses, community newspapers, public health nurses, health professionals, libraries, women's health and/or

104

resource centres, women's bookshops, Plunket rooms and doctor's surgeries (be prepared for mixed reactions from doctors). Don't forget the local anorexia/bulimia network newsletter. (Most larger cities will have one.)

Support groups require a lot of energy and effort to set up and maintain, but can be extremely rewarding. They are not a therapy situation but an opportunity for women to share their experiences and offer support to each other. Their value is in the validation of feelings and experiences ('I'm not the only one'), and the safe space they offer for talking about conflicts and difficult-to-express feelings. There's no 'expert' offering solutions, but in sharing experiences we often learn new possibilities for ourselves.

Some possible ground rules

These should be discussed within the group before being finalized and every group member should be clear about what each one means.

○ Commitment to the eight weeks, after the first session.
○ Arriving and starting on time.
○ Phone if you can't make it.
○ Confidentiality within the group.
○ Use 'I' statements (talk about yourself, not others).
○ Accept other women's feelings, rather than try to comfort them away.
○ Don't censor your own thoughts, accept the value of what you have to say.
○ Acknowledge differences and be open to what others say.
○ Listen to others when they speak.
○ Don't tell other women what they should be doing. If you have experiences to offer, present them in the form, 'I found it helpful to . . .'

The booklet *Getting Started*, by Celine Kearney, published by the Mental Health Foundation of New Zealand (see Resource section), has very useful information on setting up and running a self-help group.

9 For Friends and Relations

Being close to someone with an eating disorder can be very difficult. Try to be supportive and encouraging without making her eating disorder your problem – you cannot 'make her better'.

DO

Listen without judging.
For example, say 'That must be hard to deal with' rather than 'You're over-reacting'; 'You obviously feel really strongly about that' rather than 'Pull yourself together'. Accept and validate the feelings she has, rather than impose your judgements on them or tell her how she should feel.

Affirm things other than appearance.
'You were really warm with your father today even though he was being difficult', 'You handled that well', or 'You have been really patient with your sick child'. Notice when she is feeling good about herself and reinforce this.

Encourage communication about feelings.
'Do you want to talk some more about being angry?' Use open-ended questions like 'Tell me some more about . . .'

Show that you care.
Be as warm and supportive as you can without making the way she is the focus of all your attention. Ask her to do things for you, e.g. 'I have a headache, would you give me a neck rub?' or, 'I'd like to go to a movie/out visiting/for a walk, would you like to come?'

Love her for what she is, not how she looks.
'I like the way you talk to the cat/handle your work/laugh at TV . . .' Focus your attention as well as your comments on things other than her appearance.

Share your concerns about her eating patterns.
'It bothers me that you don't eat dinner.' Encourage her to talk about how she feels about it, but avoid getting obsessive and talking about it too frequently.

Explore what is going on in all aspects of her life.
'What sort of day did you have at work?' or, 'How did the
visit to your brother's go?'

Be direct in your communication.
Say you are angry/worried/unhappy rather than giving
indirect messages like banging cupboards, looking at her
anxiously, crying and then saying 'It's all right'.

Give the help she *wants.*
If she says she wants you to not buy certain foods, not to
expect her to eat out for a while, not to ask her parents to
visit, etc, respect this. Don't 'know better' what is good for
her.

Put most of your energy into your own life.
Her own obsession with food and eating is hard enough for
her to deal with. Don't add yours to it. Being concerned and
supportive is different from watching her every move and
wanting to know what she has eaten every day.

Support small steps and changes.
We often feel threatened by changes in someone we are close
to and act in ways that will push them back to the way they
have always been. Try and deal with your own fears.

Let her establish her own ideals and values.
This is often particularly difficult for parents. But think back
to your own experience, did you agree with all *your* parents'
ideas?

Encourage independence, initiative and autonomy
'That's a good idea' rather than 'You'll never be able to
afford to go flatting!' When she asks you not to treat her in a
certain way (for example, putting your arm around her in
public in a proprietorial way, indicating that she is 'your'
woman), take notice of what she says.

Learn about the wider context in which eating disorders exist
– read this book, particularly Chapter 1.

Acknowledge your own feelings and deal with them yourself.
If you find it difficult to treat your 'little girl' as grown up,
look at why this is and work towards changing it. If you are
feeling threatened by your partner becoming more assertive,
look at why this is and explore ways of being more direct
and clear in your own behaviour.

For men – learn the skills of relating and communication.
Have you learnt that it's 'unmanly' to express feelings, or talk
about the things that concern you personally? Do you avoid
or feel impatient when she wants to talk about how she feels?
Think about this and what rewards there could be for you in
dropping this defensiveness.

Show love and affection in ways that she likes.
When she says 'I'd like a hug', give her just that rather than
assuming she means sex.

DON'T

Monitor her eating – let it be her responsibility.
Avoid noticing or commenting on what she eats (or doesn't)
every day. Don't ask "what have you eaten today".

Comment on weight loss or gain.
This is probably a big problem for her. Avoid reinforcing it.

Comment on appearance and nothing else.
'You look happy/excited' is much better than a comment on
appearance.

Make put-down remarks of any sort.

Use emotional blackmail.
For example, 'Your mother and I have agreed that we will
xxxx when you lose some weight' or, 'You'll feel better in
summer if you can wear a bikini'. (Real meaning: *I'll* feel
better.)

Make loving anyone conditional on how she looks.

Make the decision about seeking help for anyone else.

Arrange appointments for someone else.

Try to persuade her to eat.

Threaten or 'wave a big stick' to try to make her change.

Focus on food or eating all the time.

Dominate.

Guilt-trip.

Know best.

Make decisions for her.

Assume that you are always right.

Expect to be able to handle the situation perfectly.

Blame yourself for her behaviour.

Compare her with other members of the family (or your ex-wife).

Force anyone to eat.

Expect her to share all your values.

Expect there to be ready answers.

Be a martyr.

See it as a disease.

Behave 'like a man' – be detached, authoritative, uninvolved.

Neglect the other people in your life.

When we are close to anyone with an identifiable 'problem', we often tend to blame them for everything that is wrong in our own lives. It becomes a way for us to avoid taking responsibility for our own feelings, actions and life. The most helpful thing you can do is be loving and supportive *without* making her eating disorder or appearance the total focus of your life. Treat her like a fully grown-up and functioning person.

FOOTNOTES

1. Jasbindar's research and its results are described in 'I'm Eating My Heart Out', *Broadsheet*, October 1987, New Zealand.
2. Described in 'I'm Eating My Heart Out', *Broadsheet*,
3. Judy Norsigian of the Boston Women's Health Collective writing in *Network News*.
4. HC Lowe, SW Miler and CG Richards, 'Eating Attitudes in an Adolescent Schoolgirl Population', *NZ Medical Journal*, 8 May 1985.
5. Described in 'I'm Eating My Heart Out', *Broadsheet*,
6. D Garner and P Garfinkle, *Handbook of Psychotherapy for Anorexia Nervosa and Bulimia*, The Guilford Press, New York.
7. Quotes from *Self Help with PMS*, Michelle Harrison, Random House, 1982.
8. Statements from an article by Dr Anne Hall in *Modern Medicine of New Zealand*, August 1984.
9. From *A Preventative Curriculum for Anorexia Nervosa and Bulimia*, The Bulimia Anorexia Association, Faculty of Human Kinetics, University of Windsor, Ontario, Canada.
10. Adapted from *Eating Disorders*, ed Jill Elka Harkaway, The Family Therapy Collective, Aspen Public., Maryland, USA.
11. From *Eating Disorders*, above.

Resources

Groups and Contacts

UK AND IRELAND
Anorexia Anonymous, 24 Westmoreland Road, London SW13. (081) 748 3994
Anorexia and Bulimia Nervosa Association, London. (071) 885 3936
Anorexic Aid, The Priory Centre, 11 Priory Road, High Wycombe, Bucks. (0494) 21431
Anorexic Aid, Hinchogue Cottage, Carrickmines, Co Dublin.
Anorexia Family Aid and National Information Centre, Sackville Place, 44 Sackville Street, Norwich, Norfolk NR3 1JE. (0603) 621414
Compulsive Eating Groups, c/o The Women's Therapy Centre, 6 Manor Gardens, London N7. (071) 263 6200
Outreach Anorexia, c/o 84 University Street, Belfast BT7 1HE. (084) 228474
Overeaters Anonymous, Dublin. (01) 694800 ext 250
Overeaters Anonymous, c/o Bryson House, 28 Bedford Street, Belfast.
Overeaters Anonymous, PO Box 19, Streatford, Manchester H32 9EB. (061) 868 4109
Turning Point, Positive Health Care Centre, 2 Lansdown Gardens, Shelbourne Road, Dublin 4. (01) 680588

Useful Reading

Many books have been published on food problems now. We think the best are those that come from a feminist perspective. Be wary of any that suggest that it's no more than a personal problem, or that have an underlying assumption that what they suggest will make you thinner.

GENERAL
Bruch, Hilda. *The Golden Cage: The Enigma of Anorexia Nervosa* Open Books, 1978
Cannon, Geoffrey & Hetty Einzeig. *Dieting Makes You Fat* Century, 1983

Chapkis, Wendy. *Beauty Secrets: Women and the Politics of Appearance* The Women's Press, 1986
Chernin, Kim. *Womansize: The Tyranny of Slenderness* The Women's Press, 1983
Chernin, Kim. *The Hungry Self: Women, Eating and Identity* Virago, 1986
Hutchinson, Marcia Germaine. *Transforming Body Image (Learning to Love the Body You Have)* The Crossing Press, 1985
Kovals, Ramona. *Eating Your Heart Out* Penguin, 1986
Lawrence, Marilyn. *The Anorexic Experience* The Women's Press, 1984
Lawrence, Marilyn (ed). *Fed Up and Hungry: Women, Oppression and Food* The Women's Press, 1987
McCarthy, Aine. *Body Matters for Women* Attic Press, 1989
Orbach, Susie. *Fat is a Feminist Issue* Arrow, 1988
Orbach, Susie. *Hunger Strike* Faber and Faber, 1986
Roth, Gennen. *Breaking Free from Compulsive Eating* Grafton, 1986

PREMENSTRUAL SYNDROME
Duckworth, Helen. *Premenstrual Syndrome: Your Options* Attic Press, 1990

SEXUAL ABUSE
Danica, Elly. *Don't: A Woman's Word* Attic Press, 1989
Liddy, Rosemary & Deirdre Walsh. *Surviving Sexual Abuse* Attic Press, 1988

SELF-HELP GROUPS
Krzowski, Sue & Pat Land. *In Our Experience: Workshops at the Women's Therapy Centre* Attic Press, 1988

SEXUALITY
Kitzinger, Sheila. *Women's Experience of Sex* Penguin, 1985
Maher, Chi. *Sex Education and Health Matters for Girls* Attic Press, 1990